IRAQ STRATEGY REVIEW

Options for U.S. Policy

• • •

Edited by Patrick L. Clawson

• • •

Contributors:
Daniel L. Byman
Michael J. Eisenstadt
John Hillen
Andrew T. Parasiliti
Kenneth M. Pollack

• • •

A Washington Institute Monograph

• • •

THE WASHINGTON INSTITUTE FOR NEAR EAST POLICY

© 1998 by the Washington Institute for Near East Policy

Published in 1998 in the United States of America by the Washington Institute for Near East Policy, 1828 L Street NW, Suite 1050, Washington, DC 20036.

Library of Congress Cataloging-in-Publication Data

Iraq strategy review : options for U.S. policy / edited by Patrick L.
    Clawson ; contributors, Daniel L. Byman ... [et al.].
            p.   cm.
        ISBN 0-944029-26-4
        1. United States—Foreign relations—Iraq. 2. Iraq—
    Foreign relations—United States. 3. United States—Foreign
    relations—1989– I. Clawson, Patrick L., 1951–   . II.
    Byman, Daniel, 1967–   . III. Washington Institute for Near
    East Policy.
    E183.8.I57I73   1988
    327.730567—dc21   98-23817
                                                                  CIP
Cover design concept by Naylor Design Inc.

CONTENTS

ACKNOWLEDGMENTS

In preparing this monograph, the Washington Institute convened a pair of review boards to critique the various essays and offer comments, criticism, and guidance to the authors. Geoffrey Kemp, Zalmay Khalilzad, Samuel Lewis, Alan Makovsky, and Robert Pelletreau participated in these review boards, and the authors and the Institute would like to thank them for their sage advice while exonerating them for any of the opinions expressed herein.

Paul Wolfowitz generously reviewed sections of the final product and provided us with the insight of his wisdom and experience. Max Singer provided detailed assistance in clarifying what the analytical framework of "Liberation" assumes and what policies could be adopted to support the Iraqi people in liberating themselves.

Elyse Aronson, Monica Hertzman, Jonathan Lincoln, Amir Nahai, and Leah Thomas furnished invaluable assistance researching, editing and preparing this volume.

PREFACE

More than seven years after the Gulf War, Saddam Husayn continues to flout UN Security Council resolutions with increasing frequency and boldness. Meanwhile, Washington struggles to hold together the Gulf War coalition and yet find some way to respond to Baghdad's constant challenges. At the same time, many of America's allies are growing restless with containment. Sanctions fatigue has set in and there are growing calls for the lifting of sanctions on Iraq. At home, many Americans are frustrated by Washington's inability to "get rid" of Saddam or to find a more permanent solution to the problem posed by Iraq.

Together, these forces have generated a heated debate in Washington over U.S. policy toward Iraq. Inside the government, leading politicians and diplomats are reexamining America's Iraq policy to decide whether it should be bolstered or changed. On the outside, experts, analysts, and commentators of every persuasion provide voices offering new strategies toward Iraq.

The problem with Iraq is that, like many foreign policy issues, each option entails advantages and disadvantages, costs, risks, and tradeoffs. The key for policymakers and for the American people is to decide which policy offers the best possibility of securing U.S interests in the Persian Gulf. To answer that question, one must understand what each policy would entail. Unfortunately, snappy slogans and empty phrases too often substitute for analysis of policy options. *Iraq Strategy Review* is designed to try to fill this gap.

Iraq Strategy Review introduces a new type of publication from The Washington Institute. In response to the debate over Iraq policy, the Institute commissioned five experts to delve into the range of strategies the United States could pursue. Each of the essays in this volume looks at a different potential approach America can take toward Iraq. Each of these essays provides a detailed analysis of the option, focusing on its strengths, its weaknesses, and the requirements to implement it. Each of these essays is presented as if in response to the question, "How could the United States implement this policy?"

Iraq Strategy Review is intended as a guide for perplexed policymakers charged with improving or changing America's current Iraq policy. Each option is examined in great detail, but none is specifically endorsed. That is because the purpose of this exercise is to inform the policy debate, not to direct it. While reaffirming the merits of prescriptions offered in other Institute publications—including the 1996 final report of the Presidential Study Group—we present *Iraq Strategy Review* with the more modest hope that it might provide a solid foundation on which to build future policy toward a vitally important issue.

<table>
<tr><td>Mike Stein
President</td><td>Barbi Weinberg
Chairman</td></tr>
</table>

CONTRIBUTORS

Daniel L. Byman is a policy analyst with the RAND Corporation specializing in Middle East politics, the use of aerospace power, and terrorism. He has served as a Persian Gulf political analyst at the Central Intelligence Agency.

Patrick L. Clawson is director for research at The Washington Institute for Near East Policy and senior editor of *Middle East Quarterly*. Previously, he was a senior research professor at the Institute for National Strategic Studies of the National Defense University and editor of INSS's flagship annual publication, *Strategic Assessment*.

Michael J. Eisenstadt is a senior fellow at The Washington Institute. He is the author most recently of *'Knives, Tanks, and Missiles': Israel's Security Revolution* (Washington Institute, 1998).

John Hillen is the Olin Fellow for National Security Studies at the Washington office of the Council on Foreign Relations. A former U.S. Army reconnaissance officer and paratrooper, he fought in the 1991 Persian Gulf War with the Second Armored Cavalry Regiment.

Andrew Parasiliti is director of programs at the Middle East Institute. He specializes in Iraqi politics and Persian Gulf security issues.

Kenneth M. Pollack is a research fellow at the Washington Institute specializing in political and military affairs of the Persian Gulf states. He has worked in Near East and South Asian affairs at the National Security Council and was a Persian Gulf military analyst at the Central Intelligence Agency.

RETHINKING IRAQ STRATEGY
Why and How?

Patrick L. Clawson

Iraq has been a continuing problem for U.S. policy, as was brought home during the November 1997–February 1998 crisis. Whereas much dissatisfaction was heard about the current policy, the popular debate exposed the difficulties with alternative courses of action. The aim of this study is to flesh out that policy debate by presenting the detailed case for each of the policy alternatives.

REVIEWING THE PRESENT SITUATION

The challenge posed by Iraq for U.S. policy has some enduring elements, but it has also changed rather significantly in the last two years.

What Has Remained the Same?

Iraq under President Saddam Husayn continues to pose a major challenge to Middle East peace and stability. As Bruce Riedel, the National Security Council's senior director for Near East and South Asian affairs, told The Washington Institute, "We all know it is not over. Saddam Husayn's track record is all too clear. He will continue to challenge the international community because his goals remain regional domination and revenge for past defeats. That is why he started two wars and tried to assassinate President Bush and the emir of Kuwait."[1]

Nothing brings out more sharply the severity of the Iraq threat than the issue of weapons of mass destruction (WMD) and the missiles with which to deliver them. Whereas many nations have WMD arsenals, Iraq is the only one with a recent track record of using them not once but several times. In both wars it started, Saddam's Iraq has employed ballistic missiles—against Tehran, Tel Aviv, Riyadh, and Manama. It repeatedly used chemical weapons in the war against Iran and against its own people in the Anfal campaigns of the late 1980s, and reports by weapons inspectors of the United Nations Special Commission on Iraq (UNSCOM) indicate clearly that Iraq had plans to use chemical weapons in the second Gulf war until it was deterred by the threat of retaliation from the U.S.-led coalition. Given this track record, the UN Security Council imposed unique and far-reaching restrictions on Iraq's WMD program in the form of Resolution 687. Yet, rather than comply with the will of the international community, Saddam has forgone $110 billion in oil income. The willingness to forgo that much money is a frightening indicator of how much Saddam values his remaining WMD capabilities.

To be certain, much has been accomplished in containing the Iraqi threat. UNSCOM weapons inspections have uncovered and reduced much of Iraq's WMD capabilities, achieving far more in this regard than did the 1991 Gulf War. Sanctions have stripped Iraq of the economic, political, and military influence it enjoyed before the Gulf War. The ban on general trade has prevented Iraq from acquiring materials to restore its military–industrial base and has severely limited clandestine arms acquisition, while the general atmosphere of privation caused by sanctions has contributed to the widespread demoralization of the armed forces. The UN Security Council continues to support sanctions and weapons inspections, and America's Gulf allies continue to support the U.S. military presence. At the same time, Iraq has not complied with many of the forty-plus relevant UN Security Council resolutions adopted since 1990.

What Has Changed?

Internationally, support for strong measures to contain Iraq appears to be slipping. Saddam can reasonably believe that time is on his side, that he is slowly returning to the community of nations without having to change his policy in the ways the United States has insisted since 1990. He can look with satisfaction at the respect he is accorded by UN secretary-general Kofi Annan, who both judged Saddam a man with whom he could work and criticized UNSCOM for its over-rigidity. Russia, France, and many Arab countries take Saddam's side in debates about the future of sanctions and weapons inspections. Meanwhile, in the wake of the crisis of November 1997–February 1998, Saddam may have concluded that the U.S. threat to use force, which seems to have compelled Iraq to cease obstructions in the past, has become less credible.

On the most highly publicized issue—namely WMDs—the will of the international community to follow this issue through is in question. The result of the 1997–1998 crisis was to allow resumption of UNSCOM inspections, whereas Iraq did nothing toward fulfilling its responsibility to provide information about its weapons program. In other words, Saddam agreed only to let UNSCOM resume searching the haystack for the WMD needle, whereas Resolution 687 requires him actually to produce the needle. There is talk—if the inspectors find nothing—of closing at least the nuclear file and moving toward less intrusive monitoring rather than active inspection, even though Iraq has not produced complete evidence about what it did in the past and what happened to the material and personnel working on those programs. This could raise doubts about the credibility of the United Nations in dealing with the threat of WMD proliferation—a problem the world is certain to face even more starkly in coming years.

Furthermore, the economic containment of Iraq is leaking. Saddam has deprived his own people to curry support for ending sanctions; he has used the world's concern for protecting the people of Iraq to protect his weapons of mass destruction.

His propaganda has convinced many that Iraqis are starving to death, whereas his own government admits that the country's population has grown by more than 3 million people since 1991, at a near-record rate of growth. Responding in large part to exaggerated reports about severe privation, the UN Security Council in February 1998 adopted Resolution 1153, under which Iraq is permitted to export more oil than Iraq can currently produce; the authorized exports of $10.7 billion a year exceed the $9.5 billion that Iraq exported on average each year between 1981 and 1989. While the oil-for-food program finances most of the country's civilian needs, Saddam faces few effective restrictions upon the use of the $400 million his country receives each year from oil exported via Turkey, via Iranian waters, and—without Security Council objection—via Jordan. And Iraq campaigns for the complete lifting of oil export restrictions, signing multibillion-dollar contracts with oil firms from friendly nations like Russia and France that will be effective after sanctions are lifted.

The February 1998 resolution of one crisis is not likely to be the end of America's Saddam problem. Further disagreements are likely, both with UN partners like France and Russia, who want an easing of restrictions on Iraq, and with Saddam, who remains determined to resume his drive for regional hegemony. A crisis could erupt over one of many issues: the next UN review of sanctions and weapons inspections, a movement by more of Saddam's forces into the Kurdish zone, or a rejection of the oil-for-food program in a bid to gain complete relaxation of the sanctions, to name only a few.

THE POLICY OPTIONS

Given the certainty of future problems, U.S. interests would be well served by a strategy review. An important aim would be to determine an Iraq policy based on an assessment of U.S. interests and capabilities, rather than have one forced upon America by unforeseen events. The difficulty with such a review is that it will require making some hard choices that there is a natural tendency to postpone until forced to confront. Moreover, none of the policy options are perfect. Indeed, choosing any of them will involve significant risks, and several would require jettisoning long-held positions. Perhaps, when all the advantages and disadvantages of the various alternatives are tallied, the best approach may be to muddle through as at present. Or maybe not. The mistake would be to carry on with America's present policy without having thought systematically about the alternatives. To that end, this volume sets out the following alternative policies:

BROAD CONTAINMENT—the existing U.S. policy—could be revitalized to keep in place the full panoply of restrictions on Iraq. To prevent Iraq from threatening vital U.S. interests, the present policy rests on four pillars: weapons inspections, sanctions, no-drive and no-fly zones, and the threat of use of force. Although pressures threaten each of these pillars, the policy has time and again proven more durable than critics expected, and it has accomplished much with fewer risks and potential costs than entailed by alternative policies. In addition to bolstering international support for the coalition by making tradeoffs in other foreign policy areas, steps that could be taken to reinforce the policy's four key points include (1) shoring up UN weapons inspections by including more non-Anglo-American professional staff members (while resisting efforts to politicize UNSCOM); (2) keeping tight restrictions on Iraqi imports and closing the loopholes for oil exports via Iranian waters, Turkey, and Jordan, thus ensuring that Saddam does not benefit from easing sanctions; (3) extending the no-fly and no-drive zones if Saddam takes provocative military measures; and (4) developing and announcing a credible policy on when and how force will be used.

NARROW CONTAINMENT would acknowledge that the current broader range of constraints on Iraq cannot be sustained, and thus focus on restricting Iraqi military capabilities. The United States would rely on a smaller coalition of states, rather than on the UN, and focus on the most important restrictions on Iraq, rather than on comprehensive constraints. The fundamental reason for such a shift would be a judgment that the present broad containment approach is unlikely to last much longer, necessitating a fall-back position that could be sustained as long as Saddam is in power. A narrower coalition would be created among states willing to act in the absence of a UN imprimatur and to support all necessary measures, including the use of force. The only country whose full participation in such a coalition would be essential is Kuwait, though the participation of Saudi Arabia, Jordan, and Turkey would be extremely beneficial, and the United States would solicit support from its closest allies, such as Britain and Japan. This coalition would be dedicated to sustaining at least the three most vital parts of containment: preventing Iraqi acquisition of WMDs, constraining the rebuilding of Iraqi conventional forces, and limiting Iraqi political clout. In return for international support for measures specifically focused on these issues, the United States could agree to end the current broad economic sanctions, to compromise on the standard of compliance with UNSCOM inspections, or to make sacrifices on foreign policy issues other than Iraq.

UNDERMINING Saddam's regime would involve supporting the Iraqi opposition to weaken if not destabilize Saddam's rule to the point that he is ousted, whether by assassination-cum-coup or, less plausibly, by the opposition coming to power. Support for the opposition would require (1) helping to rebuild the opposition by working with the Iraq National Congress (INC), bolstering regional opposition groups (such as Kurdish groups in the North and Shi'i groups in the South), or stimulating creation of a new opposition; (2) establishing safe havens from which the opposition can operate, using either Kuwait or, with Turkish support, Kurdish northern Iraq; (3) seducing Saddam's henchmen to turn against the regime; (4) providing the opposition with considerable military assistance, including an air umbrella against Iraqi attacks; and (5) running interference for the opposition in the diplomatic arena while simultaneously keeping Saddam tightly contained.

Alternatively, the United States might consider an explicit policy of overthrowing Saddam, replacing him with a pluralist, pro-Western opposition. Compared to the more modest policy of undermining Saddam through support to the opposition, overthrow would require a substantially larger U.S. effort, both to train and equip the opposition and to use air power—roughly on the scale of Desert Storm—to destroy much of Iraq's remaining military capabilities. An overthrow policy could create tougher diplomatic problems, including a *de facto* end to weapons inspections, and runs the risk that Saddam will lash out with WMDs (including against Iraqis) and/or that Iraq will dissolve into chaos.

In addition, this volume considers an alternative model of supporting the Iraqi opposition based on a wholly different set of assumptions about the strength of the existing opposition relative to Saddam's regime. Supporting Iraqi liberation rests on an analytical framework which, unlike that underlying the rest of the volume, argues that a well-organized national opposition coalition—the INC—is already operating, that Saddam's army is weak relative to the opposition, and that an armed opposition force could readily defeat the regime. Given such an analysis of events inside Iraq, the recommended policy would be to provide the Iraqi opposition with enough help so it can overthrow the Ba'th regime, if that is what it is determined to do. As people in Iraq and throughout the region believe that the United States is the single biggest determinant of whether Saddam and the Ba'th can be overthrown, strong U.S. political support for the INC would dramatically improve its chances. The INC strategy would be to use modest U.S. material aid to create a mobile infantry force armed with man-portable anti-tank weapons. Protected by a U.S.-enforced ban on Iraqi flights, the INC force would take border areas (the Kurdish areas in the North, the Shi'i areas of the South, and the unpopulated West) and establish a provisional government. Cut off from the flow of oil money, Saddam would lose much of his ability to threaten or influence at home and abroad. Fueled by oil money and manpower from defecting soldiers, the INC could gradually liberate the country. Success would be a major triumph for U.S. interests, with a pluralist, pro-Western government in Iraq. But this policy is a gamble: If the key assumptions undergirding it are unfounded, the INC might find itself in a debacle that would seriously hurt U.S. interests in the region.

DETERRENCE would largely limit itself to preventing Iraqi use of force, without the current level of emphasis on restricting Iraqi military capabilities. Also, accepting that Saddam is likely to remain in power and that UN sanctions can be sustained only at a high political price, the United States would deemphasize Iraq as a foreign policy issue. Should Iraq use military force or terrorism against U.S. allies or interests, the United States would respond with swift and intense military force. While retaining a tripwire force in Kuwait, the U.S. military presence would be largely over the horizon, with periodic exercises signaling the U.S. commitment and ability to deter Iraqi aggression. Rather than emphasize a special arms control regime for Iraq, U.S. diplomacy would deal with the Iraqi problem in the context of a global counterproliferation strategy. U.S. military planners would not lose sleep over any Iraqi plan to waste money rebuilding its conventional military capabilities. Iraqi oil would be welcomed back on the world market, which could benefit U.S. consumers by prolonging the current period of low energy prices.

INVASION AND OCCUPATION would be the most ambitious U.S. option. It is realistic only in response to a significant Iraqi provocation, and only if the operation enjoyed strong congressional and U.S. public support, active cooperation from key regional allies, and at least tolerance from the broader international community. The military operations could take three to seven months with significant U.S. casualties (for example, 1,000 killed), a number that would rise if there were wild-card scenarios like WMD use or street-to-street fighting in major cities. The more difficult task would be creating a sustainable Iraqi government, pledged to international norms and a peaceful coexistence with its neighbors. This could take three to six years and would entail a short, direct U.S. occupation and a longer period of rule by an international transitional authority, to rebuild Iraq's public institutions in stages while the U.S. military retained responsibility for public order and the security of the borders.

HOW TO DECIDE WHICH POLICY IS BEST

The aim of this study is to illuminate the choices the United States faces regarding Iraq. To that end, the authors have accented the differences among the options they present. The choice among options is not necessarily so stark: Some combinations of elements from the five policies are quite possible. For instance, the deemphasis on Iraq as a foreign policy issue and the shift toward a more over-the-horizon military posture, as proposed under the deterrence option, could be matched with the measures proposed under the broad containment option to strengthen support for weapons inspections. But there is an internal logic to each of the positions; they are not "à la carte restaurant menus" from which elements can be combined at random. In particular, the stronger the U.S. support for undermining Saddam, the less plausible his acquiescence in international weapons inspections and the more problems the United States may face in securing UN support for a tough stance. Unilateral use of military force, without explicit Security Council approval, may also complicate America's ability to sustain broad international support, though that could depend upon the circumstances (for example, Washington would not suffer much, if at all, were it to act when Security Council approval was blocked by only one permanent member at a time when others on the council felt action was warranted).

Each of the policy options examined is likely to have its supporters among policymakers and analysts—that is, no one option is so clearly superior to all the others that it will command near-unanimous support. All agree that Saddam is a threat. The question is how to deal with him. One's preference will likely depend on a variety of factors, including how much of a threat Saddam is perceived to pose, how one assesses the resilience of Saddam and his regime, the importance assigned to Iraq compared to other issues (foreign or domestic), and the degree of importance attached to international support for U.S. policy.

Those who worry that Saddam could easily rebuild his WMD stockpiles if restrictions were relaxed, that he could regain regional influence and military might were sanctions eased, and that he is eager to pursue regional domination and revenge, are probably more likely to support the more activist policy options.

Judgments about the stability of Saddam's rule have a more complex effect. Those who think Saddam is politically isolated at home and may soon be overthrown may prefer to muddle through with existing policy, on the grounds that the current policy mix is sustainable for the short time Saddam will be in power, or they might prefer strong measures to overthrow him, on the theory that the United States should position itself to take credit for what is going to happen anyway.

Opinions about the relative weight to give to the Saddam problem also depend upon the evaluation of the importance of the other issues facing the United States. Many Americans might say that domestic social issues merit more attention. Even among foreign policy issues, it is not clear how high to rate the Iraq threat. After all, energy security has not been much of a problem for the last decade, and the United States gets less than ten percent of its total oil from the Gulf. Plus, were Iran and the United States to reestablish normal relations, perhaps Iraq could be kept in check largely by its neighbors, with limited U.S. assistance.

Many in the international community would prefer a less vigorous stance toward the Iraq problem. That may be a weighty consideration for those who place greater importance on achieving consensus with other governments. Those who think the UN is key for legitimizing U.S. actions that might otherwise look hegemonic are likely to be unenthusiastic about downplaying the UN role, as implicit in the narrow containment and undermine options. A related concern is that the difference between Europe and the United States about how to handle difficult regimes will eventually include Iraq, on which there has generally been more agreement than over Iran and Libya. Dispute over engagement versus containment, and about how much trade and investment should be affected by political decisions, could affect the issue, now being actively discussed, of NATO's role outside its traditional theater. Those who see the differences in approach to difficult regimes as a major problem in transatlantic relations may be less enthusiastic about narrowing the Iraq coalition. So too may those worried about popular antipathy to U.S. policy in Gulf Cooperation Council (GCC) countries, although it is not clear how much weight to give such views, given that decisions in these countries are made by monarchs.

This study is not the place to analyze how great is the Saddam threat, how resilient is his regime, how significant is the Saddam quandry relative to other problems, or how important is the breadth of international support. This is a descriptive rather than prescriptive study; its purpose is to analyze the actions required for and the implications of each policy option regarding Iraq. Every author approached his chapter in that spirit, presenting the best case for the respective policy, regardless of his own opinion on the matter.

In early 1997, The Washington Institute did provide an answer to the policy question in the final report of its Presidential Study Group, *Building for Security and Peace in the Middle East: An American Agenda.* Thirty-seven of the thirty-nine distinguished analysts and former policymakers in the group agreed with this statement: "The most urgent change needed in U.S. Middle East policy is to take steps that hasten the demise of Saddam Husayn's regime while preserving Iraq's national unity and territorial integrity." The policy they recommended included declaring that sanctions could not be lifted until after a regime change in Baghdad, outlining incentives for Iraq in the event of Saddam's ouster, and adopting more assertive military responses to Iraqi provocations. Regional and international developments since then may lead some to say that these recommendations are all the more urgent, whereas others may argue that those proposals have been overtaken by events. Neither this book's authors nor the Institute wishes to speculate what policy toward Iraq the members of the Presidential Study Group would recommend if they assembled again. It seems likely, however, that they would restate their conclusion, "It is in the interest of the United States to clarify its objectives and take the initiative now, . . . rather than permit Saddam to determine the pace and direction of events."[2] This is what *Iraq Strategy Review* is designed to do.

NOTES

[1]   Bruce O. Riedel, special assistant to the president and National Security Council senior director for Near East and South Asian affairs, "U.S. Policy in the Gulf: Five Years of Dual Containment," speech at the annual Soref Symposium of The Washington Institute for Near East Policy, Washington, D.C., May 6, 1998.

[2]   *Building for Security and Peace in the Middle East: An American Agenda,* report of the Presidential Study Group (Washington, D.C.: The Washington Institute for Near East Policy, 1997), pp. xi–xii.

Chapter 1

CONTAIN BROADLY

Bolstering America's Current Iraq Policy

Michael J. Eisenstadt

Amerca's current broad containment policy toward Iraq has—despite repeated challenges—endured and been reasonably successful at achieving certain U.S. objectives. Broad containment has sought to limit Baghdad's ability to threaten its neighbors and U.S. interests, while creating conditions in Iraq that might lead to a military coup or the overthrow of Saddam Husayn and his regime. This approach was initially based on several assumptions:

- Saddam Husayn was "irredeemable" and all efforts to integrate Iraq peacefully into the family of nations were bound to fail as long as he remained in power.

- After invading Iran in 1980 and Kuwait in 1990, there would be broad international support for a policy of containment as long as Saddam Husayn and his regime remained in power.

- Containment could limit Iraq's ability to threaten vital U.S. interests as long as necessary, or at least until Saddam was overthrown.

- Because the supply of oil would continue to outstrip world demand for years to come, the world energy market would not be a source of pressure for lifting the ban on Iraqi oil sales.

- Weapons inspections are the best way to dismantle Iraq's weapons of mass destruction (WMD) programs; in this regard, military strikes have only limited utility.

America's embrace of containment was also rooted in a recognition that, despite its shortcomings, containment was the only viable way for the United States to safeguard its vital interests in the Gulf. Alternative policies—a balance of power approach, working with the opposition to overthrow Saddam Husayn, or a ground invasion to crush his regime—were either unworkable, unattainable, or unlikely to garner the domestic and international support needed to succeed.

Despite recent problems, the policy of broad containment remains viable. There is still broad international support for the basic objectives of containment: to disarm Saddam and to ensure that he cannot rebuild his military capabilities. Moreover, under the current containment regime, the United States has the ability to veto the lifting of sanctions (however politically undesirable this might be). Finally, any attempt to seriously alter or replace the current framework, without any viable alternative policy framework to replace it, could cause grave harm to U.S. interests in the region.

DESCRIPTION OF THE POLICY

The policy of broad containment rests on four pillars: weapons inspections, sanctions, no-drive and no-fly zones in northern and southern Iraq, and the threat or use of force—to compel Baghdad to cease its obstruction of weapons inspections or to deter it from threatening its neighbors or vital U.S. interests.

Weapons Inspections

United Nations (UN) weapons inspections have played a crucial role in uncovering and reducing Iraq's WMD capabilities, achieving far more in this regard than did the coalition air campaign during the 1991 Gulf War. Experience in Iraq has shown that there is no substitute for inspectors on the ground, with the mandate to go anywhere anytime, and that on-site detection methods are much more effective at discovering proscribed weapons activities than are remote sensing capabilities. Finally, the presence of foreign inspectors on the ground, and the possibility of surprise, no-notice inspections, complicates Iraqi efforts to engage secretly in proscribed weapons-work, and constrains Iraqi activities in this domain. Iraq has acceded to the dismantling of its WMD capabilities only grudgingly and under duress. What cooperation has occurred, can be attributed to two factors: First, Baghdad hoped that limited cooperation would both enable it to make the case that it is in compliance with its obligations and to undermine international support for sanctions before its WMD arsenal could be dismantled. Second, Saddam Husayn feared that blatant obstruction would prompt military action by the United States that could threaten the stability of his regime. Thus, sanctions and the threat or use of force have been key to the success of the inspection regime. Accordingly, a weakening of either the sanctions regime or the credibility of the threat to use force would undercut the effectiveness of the inspection regime.

Sanctions

Sanctions have stripped Iraq of the political, economic, and military influence it enjoyed before the 1991 Gulf War, and they have therefore had an important impact on curtailing Iraq's troublemaking potential. By limiting imports and smuggling, sanctions help efforts to dismantle and monitor Iraq's WMD-related infrastructure. Without sanctions, the inspections and monitoring effort would be much less effective—and might not survive at all. Thus, inspections and sanctions have a mutually reinforcing effect. Sanctions have helped contain Iraq in several other ways:

- The ban on arms transfers has prevented Iraq from rebuilding its conventional forces by replacing war losses, modernizing aging equipment, or acquiring spare parts.
- The ban on unrestricted trade has prevented Iraq from acquiring parts and materials to restore its military–industrial base, keeping military production far below prewar levels.

- The general atmosphere of privation and hardship in Iraq caused by sanctions has contributed to the widespread demoralization of the armed forces, leaving only the Republican Guard and a few regular divisions to be relied on in case of war.

- The armed forces suffer from critical shortcomings—poor maintenance, severe deficiencies in the logistical system, a lack of spares, and low morale—that degrade their ability to engage in sustained combat. None of these problems are likely to be rectified as long as sanctions remain in place.

- The prospect of sanctions being eased or lifted has caused Baghdad to cooperate—albeit selectively and grudgingly—in the dismantling of its WMD programs.

- The ban on oil sales has denied Iraq the funds for equipment needed to resume large-scale production of nonconventional weapons—although Iraq's residual capabilities in this area, particularly relating to biological warfare, remain significant.

- The exclusion of Iraqi oil from world markets has ensured moderate oil prices (as distinct from low oil prices), allowing America's Gulf allies to preserve a higher income— at a time of increased social stress—than would have been possible had Iraq pumped substantial quantities of oil for the world market.

No-Drive and No-Fly Zones

The imposition of a no-drive zone in southern Iraq and a no-fly zone in the southern and central parts of the country have increased the margin of early warning available to parry future threats to Kuwait and Saudi Arabia. Key Iraqi ground units must travel a significant distance before reaching Kuwait—buying the United States additional days or even weeks in which to respond to an emerging Iraqi threat. Likewise, the no-fly zones in northern and southern Iraq allow the United States to monitor developments on the ground throughout much of the country and provide Washington with early warning of Iraqi preparations to threaten the Kurdish enclave in the North or Kuwait or Saudi Arabia to the South. The no-fly zones also constrain the Iraqi Air Force's ability to conduct flight training, and the daily violation of Iraqi air space is a constant reminder to the Iraqi military that the ruinous policies of Saddam Husayn have led to the partial loss of their country's sovereignty.

The Threat or Use of Force

Finally, the threat or use of force has, on several occasions, compelled Iraq to cease obstructing UN weapons inspectors and deterred Iraq from reasserting control over northern Iraq or from again invading its neighbors. This policy has been helped by the dramatic increase since 1991 in pre-positioned U.S. military materiel and forward-deployed forces, as well as by greater access to military facilities in friendly states in the region.

On all but one of the occasions that a confrontation with the UN Special Commission on Iraq (UNSCOM) has led to the threatened use of force by the United States, Iraq has backed down. Moreover, in October 1994, when Saddam began moving Republican Guard divisions toward Kuwait, he quickly backed off after powerful U.S. forces were sent to the Gulf. Thus, the threat or use of force has been a crucial part of U.S. efforts to contain Iraq.

The Erosion of the Four Pillars of Containment

These four pillars of U.S. policy, however, have been coming under growing pressure and have been eroded in recent years. Iraq has undermined the effectiveness of UN weapons inspections through deception, concealment, and obstruction. In addition, it has succeeded in shifting from Baghdad to UNSCOM the onus for proving whether Baghdad's WMD programs have

been dismantled (in other words, instead of Iraq having to provide information concerning those WMD capabilities for which
UNSCOM cannot account, UNSCOM must prove that Iraq is
still hiding such capabilities). This raises the likelihood that,
if time passes without any new WMD-related discoveries by
UNSCOM, there will be growing pressure to lift the ban on
Iraqi oil exports—if not the entire sanctions regime.

The desire of France, Russia, and China to recoup out-
standing debts from Iraq, and growing international concern
(particularly in the Arab world) about the impact of sanctions
on the Iraqi people, have prompted the passing of UN Security Council Resolutions 986 and 1153 which enable Iraq to
obtain "food for oil." Under Resolution 1153, Iraq is now allowed to export much oil as it did before it invaded Kuwait.
Because of technical constraints, it will be some time before
Iraq is able to produce this quantity of oil, but under 1153 it
will be allowed to import the equipment necessary for it to do
so. Sanctions have been significantly eased, and Iraq may be
able to import proscribed items under the cover of imports for
its oil and electrical sector. Moreover, the increase in oil exports are intended to reduce pressure on the UN and the United
States to lift sanctions, but they may not succeed in doing so,
whereas Iraq will be able to divert funds formerly used for
food subsidies to pay for arms smuggling, sanctions busting,
and paying off supporters of the regime. Thus, from the point
of view of maintaining the current broad containment of Iraq,
Resolution 1153 is, at best, a mixed blessing with a significant
downside.

BOLSTERING CONTAINMENT

What can the United States do to bolster its flagging containment policy? Barring a misstep by Saddam, sustaining containment will require a major diplomatic effort. The United
States will have to make Iraq one of its highest foreign policy

priorities and it will have to make difficult compromises in areas that other key countries consider vital (for example, to accomodate Russia, on Bosnia or North Atlantic Treaty Organization [NATO] expansion; to accomodate China, on Taiwan). Although such policy compromises are probably a necessary condition for sustaining the coalition, they may not, in the long term, be sufficient to keep the coalition together.

Coalition Management

Keeping the coalition intact is both the most difficult and the most important single thing that can be done to bolster the current containment of Iraq, for the simple reason that, by its very nature, broad containment requires a coalition approach. The authority for sanctions and weapons inspections is grounded in Resolution 687 and several other key resolutions. Consequently, the support of the Permanent Five (P-5) members of the UN Security Council and other key states (such as Egypt) is crucial for sanctions and inspections to succeed. For military action, the United States prefers to have the approval of the Security Council (in the form of a "material breach" resolution—which it has not obtained since 1993) and the support of key regional states for basing and staging forces (i.e., Kuwait and Saudi Arabia, and perhaps Turkey and Jordan).

In the Security Council, France, Russia, and China are sympathetic to Iraq's grievances against UNSCOM and would like to have sanctions eased or lifted expeditiously, so that they could again do business with Baghdad. These three states are thus willing to live with a degree of uncertainty regarding Iraq's residual WMD programs if it will expedite the lifting of the ban on oil sales, as provided for in paragraph 22 of Resolution 687. By contrast, the United States is not willing to accept any uncertainty at this time concerning the status of Iraq's residual WMD programs, and it wants Iraq to fulfill other UN resolutions as well before it will countenance the lifting of sanctions. Thus, there is a basic diversion in the position of the United States and other key members of the Security Council on this issue. As a result, Washington has been unable to win support for new, more restrictive resolutions against Iraq.

Washington could try to close the gap between its own position toward Baghdad and that of Paris, Moscow, and Beijing, by offering tradeoffs in other areas. Given the current investment of French and Russian diplomacy in Iraq, the United States would have to consider significant concessions to secure their support for efforts to restore containment. Conversely, it could threaten more vigorous unilateral steps—such as adopting a strategy of undermine or invade if these countries do not halt efforts to curtail inspections or lift sanctions—though this could backfire, causing France, Russia, and China to redouble their efforts to ease or lift sanctions. In any case, the United States would, whenever possible, rely on administrative delaying tactics and use the bureaucratic inertia of the UN to freeze or slow down the gradual erosion of the sanctions and inspection regimes caused by the weakening of the international coalition.

The United States faces a different set of problems regarding its coalition partners in the Middle East. America's Gulf allies fear that the United States will eventually weary of its role as regional balancer and go home, leaving them to fend for themselves against Saddam Husayn. They are thus unwilling to support U.S. military actions that arouse Saddam's desire for vengeance without dealing him a severe blow or eliminating him. The perception that America is ultimately unwilling or unable to finish off Saddam is rooted both in seven years' experience of working with the United States in the Gulf and in the logic of containment—which lacks a mechanism to rid Iraq of Saddam and his regime. It will therefore be very difficult to alter this perception. Likewise, growing popular sympathy for the plight of the Iraqi people makes it difficult for Saudi Arabia, Jordan, and the Arab Gulf countries to openly support repeated military action against Iraq. In the past, at least some of these countries would have been willing to support military action, but they wanted to know that such use of the military instrument would have decisive results; the United States was, and still is, unable to provide such assurances. Moreover, after the most recent standoff with Iraq (November 1997 to February 1998)—in which the United States expended significant diplomatic capital to gain support for a military buildup in the region that in the end did nothing to rid the world of the Iraqi dictator—America's Gulf allies are even less likely to support future military action (barring overt aggression by Baghdad). Finally, Turkey is willing to live with the current regime in Baghdad and would not mind if the Iraqi army were once again on its border, as this would make it easier to deal with Kurdistan Workers' Party (PKK) insurgents. For this reason, Turkey has been unwilling to support military action since 1991, and it is unlikely to do so in the future.

The United States can, finally, try to argue more persuasively than it has in the past that there is no alternative to containment; that even limited strikes against Iraq are in the interest of the Gulf countries, as they strengthen the ability of the international coalition to deter Saddam, but that a strong military blow would greatly diminish Saddam's ability to threaten his neighbors and is therefore in the interest of the countries that neighbor Iraq; that the United States has been at the forefront of efforts to alleviate the suffering of the Iraqi people; that sustaining containment requires the Gulf countries' continued support for inspections, sanctions, no-fly/no-drive zones, and the use of force; and that all the peoples of the region will be at risk if Saddam is allowed to rebuild his arsenal and threaten a new war—which he will do if containment is allowed to collapse.

Weapons Inspections

The UN weapons inspection and monitoring regime is crucial to preventing Iraq from rebuilding its WMD capabilities, and it should continue for at least as long as Saddam Husayn and his regime remain in power, and probably longer. (According to UN resolutions, the weapons inspection and monitoring regime is open-ended.) Although inspections have their limits—they cannot prevent Iraq from retaining a residual WMD capability that in some areas (such as biological weapons) might be quite significant—they are crucial to efforts to prevent Iraq from rebuilding its WMD capabilities beyond current levels. Inspections also make it politically impossible for Saddam to use his residual WMD capabilities—except *in extremis*. Their use would put the lie to Iraqi claims that its WMD capabilities have been destroyed and breathe new life into the inspections regime.

There are several ways the UN inspection regime might be shored up or even strengthened:

1. Actively seek out more non-Anglo–American inspectors from countries not hostile to the position of the U.S. and British governments on Iraq, thus deflecting accusations that the deck is stacked against Iraq because of the predominance of American and British weapons inspectors in UNSCOM.

2. Fight against any further changes to the organization of UNSCOM (such as occurred following the Kofi Annan–Tariq Aziz memorandum of understanding in February 1998), and refuse to allow weapons "files" to be closed sequentially. The closing of individual files is likely to generate calls by France, Russia, and China, for the incremental lifting of sanctions, and thus should be rejected. Compliance is an all-or-nothing affair.

3. Avoid making proliferation the main issue, as this opens Washington up to charges that it employs a double standard by turning a "blind eye" to Israel's nuclear program. Rather, the United States should emphasize that it is Saddam

Husayn and his regime that are the problem. In this light, efforts to disarm Iraq of its WMD are primarily a means of dealing with the threat posed by Saddam Husayn and his regime.

4. Consider steps to ensure that Iraq's stocks of radioactive isotopes are monitored. These are permitted under Resolution 707 for medical, agricultural, and industrial use, but they could also be used to make radiological weapons. Monitoring arrangements should therefore be extended to these materials.

5. Close existing loopholes in Resolution 687, under which Iraq is permitted to produce missiles with ranges less than 150km (thus enabling it to preserve the expertise required to develop missiles with longer ranges). Moreover, under 687 there is no explicit prohibition on the development or possession of cruise missiles (although UNSCOM has in practice applied the restrictions on ballistic missiles to cruise missiles as well), and the resolution implies that Iraq could be allowed, in the future, to acquire nuclear reactors that run on natural or low-enriched uranium fuel. To close these loopholes, the UN Security Council should pass a new resolution that proscribes *all* missile programs and prohibits Iraq from acquiring any type of nuclear reactor for the indefinite future. Obtaining such a new resolution will require the United States to make concessions to various Security Council member states; even then, it might be difficult to pass such a restrictive resolution in a divided council.

6. Finally, the United States might take steps to break up Iraqi weapons teams to prevent proscribed design, research, and development work, and to allow key Iraqi weapons scientists to leave the country for employment in peaceful projects overseas. This recommendation, however, is likely to prompt strong opposition from key Security Council members and the Arab states.

Sanctions

What is important about sanctions is that they deny Saddam

both the income he would need to rebuild his conventional and nonconventional military capabilities and the oil export capability that was the source of Iraq's former economic clout. Easing or lifting sanctions need not mean that Saddam will soon be able to rebuild Iraq's military capabilities—the income can instead go into an escrow fund for spending on food, humanitarian services, and reconstruction projects. The United States could do a number of things to tighten sanctions and ensure that Saddam does not benefit from their easing or lifting:

- Require Iraq to maintain pre–Resolution 986 levels of spending out of its own resources on subsidies for food and medicine for its own people. This can be a condition for renewing the increase in oil sales permitted under Resolution 1153. It would prevent the regime from deriving benefits from the "food for oil" deal.

- Maintain tight control over humanitarian oil sales permitted under Resolutions 986 and 1153 and require Iraq to stop smuggling oil via Turkey and the Gulf before the UN Security Council approves the export of additional oil extraction equipment.

- Cut off Iraqi oil shipments through Jordan, which earns Saddam some $300 million in income a year. This, however, would require the United States to find a source of cheap, subsidized oil for Jordan to compensate for its loss of access to Iraqi oil.

- Organize a more effective counterpropaganda effort to highlight Iraqi distortions concerning the harmful humanitarian impact of sanctions. In particular, avoid claims that Iraqis were "starving" before the passage of Resolutions 986 and 1153, because first, it is untrue, and second, it creates the impression, when Iraq claims that 986 and 1153 are not being implemented effectively, that people are still "starving."

No-Fly/No-Drive Zones

Although enforcing the southern no-drive zone and the northern and southern no-fly zones are resource-intensive activities, they constrain Iraq's military freedom of action and are a way of maintaining pressure on Baghdad. Should it desire to do so, the United States could ratchet up the pressure on Iraq by further extending the no-drive and no-fly zones. Specifically, it could establish a no-drive zone in northern Iraq or extend the no-fly zone to the entire country. To enforce a northern no-drive zone, however, would require Turkey to allow coalition aircraft based at Incirlik to launch air strikes at ground targets in Iraq if necessary; Ankara would be reluctant to do so, because Turkey would just as soon have the Iraqi army along its border to control areas used by the PKK. This would therefore require major concessions to Turkey (on arms sales, for instance). As for extending the no-fly zone to the entire country, this would require that aviation assets deployed to the region increase their operations tempo. Moreover, additional air assets would have to be deployed to the region, putting increased strain on U.S. forces and exposing them to increased risk, to achieve a result of questionable value.

The Threat or Use of Force

Encouraging the perception that the United States retains the ability to inflict punishing air strikes on assets that Saddam holds dear is crucial to future efforts to contain Iraq. However, if force is used, it must be employed in such a way that it does not further erode the coalition.

The United States will have to take two steps to make credible the threat to use force: First, it will have to retain sufficient cruise missiles and combat aircraft in the region to land painful blows against Iraq while ensuring—in part through increased consultation with its regional allies—that political constraints do not prevent it from using these assets, if needed.

Second, it will have to engage in counterpropaganda efforts to increase its military freedom of action. These efforts must emphasize the fact that tens or hundreds of thousands of people (most of them Iraqis) will die if Saddam is allowed to rearm and again plunge the region into war, an outcome that can be prevented through broad containment.

In considering how to bolster the containment of Iraq, the United States has to balance the potential benefits of military action against the potential harm that the use of force could cause to U.S. interests if Iraq decides to throw UNSCOM out, or if military action leads to greater pressure to lift sanctions. The United States will need to consider what it can do to reduce objections by UN Security Council members—especially France, but also China and Russia—to U.S. use of force under existing UN resolutions. Barring a rash move by Saddam, there may not be much the United States could do to convince these countries to take a more benign view of the military option.

In the wake of the November 1997–February 1998 crisis, it appears that the United States only considers threats to U.S. assets or allies as sufficient justification for the use of force, while obstruction of UNSCOM brings consultations or the threat of force—but nothing more. Such a policy will ultimately lead to the collapse of broad containment. The willingness to use force in response to the obstruction of UNSCOM—as well as in cases where U.S. assets and allies are threatened—is a critical element of broad containment. At the very least, the United States must foster the perception that it is willing to use force. If the United States decides to carry out military action, it should strike at assets that Saddam holds dear; leave him worse off afterwards than he was beforehand; and raise the possibility that military action could upset the delicate domestic balance of power in Iraq, leading to an uprising or coup. The United States has two options here:

1. *Limited missile and air strikes launched almost automatically in the event of a provocation—such as Iraqi obstruction of UN weapons inspectors.* In this case, military action must be proportionate and relevant to the provocation; thus, the United States might destroy any facility that Iraq prevents weapons inspectors from entering, or individual targets that are of value to the regime. The virtue of this approach is that, because these strikes are limited in scope and duration, the potential for collateral damage or political backlash is minimized. Likewise, the United States does not need the support of its regional allies to launch a limited strike; U.S. naval assets normally in the region are sufficient. The disadvantage is that if Saddam believes the stakes are high enough, he may simply absorb such strikes and continue as before, in which case the United States would look ineffective.

2. *Extensive, sustained missile and air strikes initiated infrequently, after consulting with America's allies, and only in response to major infractions.* The advantage of this response is that such strikes have the potential for inflicting serious damage on Iraq's military capabilities—and thus its ability to threaten its neighbors or the Kurdish enclave. Moreover, such strikes—if targeted against the organizations that ensure Saddam's survival (such as the Republican Guard and Special Republican Guard)—could potentially create the conditions for the overthrow of the regime through a coup or an uprising. The disadvantage is that such strikes have the potential for serious political damage to the coalition and to U.S. domestic support for Iraq policy, especially in the event of heavy civilian casualties. For an extensive, sustained campaign, Gulf Cooperation Council (GCC) support would be very important, though not necessarily crucial. Although the campaign might be conducted solely from several aircraft carriers, it would be much more readily accomplished if Saudi Arabia as well as Kuwait permitted logistical, reconnaissance,

and search-and-rescue support—if not basing rights for the campaign's combat aircraft.

It will be increasingly difficult in the future to exercise the military option. The constraints on American military freedom of action are growing, not diminishing. Moreover, after spending much political capital to convince various countries to join in a military coalition to confront Iraqi obstruction between November 1997 and February 1998—only to accept in the end a diplomatic solution—it will be much more difficult to convince reluctant allies to join Washington in confronting Baghdad in future crises. Therefore, the United States should attempt to anticipate Iraqi challenges and move to head them off before they reach the point at which military strikes are the only option left. Accordingly, it should lobby Paris and Moscow to press Baghdad to cooperate with UN weapons inspectors, explaining that, in the wake of the most recent standoff with Iraq, Washington will be under even greater domestic political pressure than before to use force.

END STATE

The desired end state of broad containment is to prevent Iraq from rebuilding its conventional military forces; to eliminate Iraq's WMD capabilities or at least cap them at current levels; and to maintain Iraq's relative political isolation for as long as Saddam remains in power—as it will be much more difficult to maintain weapons inspections and sanctions once Iraq is reintegrated into the international community. In the event that Saddam and his regime should pass from the scene, a successor regime must be required to comply with Resolution 687. Failure to do so should ensure the continuation of the current containment regime, though this may not be possible, and the United States might have to make do with a much more circumscribed form of containment outside of the framework of the UN.

ADVANTAGES

The current containment regime has a number of advantages:

- *It maximizes pressures and constraints on Saddam Husayn* because it consists of the most intrusive weapons inspection and the tightest sanctions regime ever.

- *It has international legitimacy and relatively broad international support,* to the degree that it is based on various UN resolutions. Moreover, because the United States has a veto at the UN, it can ultimately block steps that could undercut this policy (although there is likely to be a political price for doing so).

- *It has worked,* and it would be dangerous to abandon this approach for another policy with uncertain prospects for success. Without weapons inspections and sanctions, Iraq will be much more difficult to deal with and will pose a much greater threat to international security than it now does.

- *It is a "doable" policy—despite the growing challenges it now faces.* Containment does not aspire to an objective that is beyond America's means. Thus, there is a rough correspondence between the desired end and the means available to achieve it. And whereas there are risks and costs associated with the policy, they are not as great as the risks and costs associated with such alternatives as deterrence or invasion.

- *Although U.S. efforts to contain Iraq have strained its relations with the GCC states, France, Russia, and China, these tensions—while undesirable—are tolerable,* and they could be eased through offering various concessions to these key states in areas largely unrelated to Iraq.

- *Saddam might always do something foolish that would further delay the eventual collapse of containment.* Meanwhile, as long as inspections continue and sanctions remain in place, Saddam will remain relatively weak—and thus potentially vulnerable to a coup; new discoveries re-

lating to Iraq's WMD programs are possible—allowing
for further dismantling of these capabilities; and Iraq's
ability to threaten its neighbors will diminish, because of
the continued decline in the condition of its conventional
military forces.

LIABILITIES AND RISKS

Despite the above advantages, continuing the broad containment of Iraq has its problems:

- *There are limits to what the policy can accomplish.* While
Iraq's conventional military is much weaker than it was
before the 1991 Gulf War, it is still the largest military in
the Gulf, and if and when sanctions are lifted, it will provide a foundation for Iraq's efforts once again to transform itself into the dominant regional power. Although
sustained air strikes could further reduce Iraq's capabilities in this area, they might have a negative impact on
America's ability to ensure the integrity of the weapons
inspection and sanctions regimes. Moreover, it is now clear
that there are limits to what weapons inspections can accomplish, and Iraq will probably be able to retain a significant residual WMD capability—even if inspections and
monitoring continue. Of greatest concern here is the possibility that Iraq could produce a nuclear explosive device
or weapon—even with sanctions and inspections in
place—if it were to succeed in acquiring fissile material
from the former Soviet Union or elsewhere. Such a development would be disastrous, as Iraq might try to use such
a capability to force an end to inspections and sanctions,
or threaten its neighbors or U.S. forces in the region. A
nuclear-armed Saddam bent on revenge is a nightmare scenario that containment may not be able to prevent.
- *Containment lacks a mechanism to create an outcome in
Iraq that would serve U.S. interests.* It provides a means

for managing the threat that Saddam Husayn poses, but it does not provide a means of removing the source of the problem: Saddam Husayn and his regime.

- *The containment regime's cornerstone—Resolution 687—is self-subverting if implemented as currently framed.* Lifting the ban on Iraq's oil exports once its WMD programs have been dismantled would provide Iraq with the political and economic leverage and wherewithal to undermine the weapons monitoring regime and rebuild its WMD programs. On the other hand, a U.S. veto of the lifting of the ban would greatly complicate U.S. relations with France, Russia, and China, possibly resulting in additional problems in Iran, Bosnia, or Taiwan, or prompting one or more of these countries to actively undercut UNSCOM or ignore sanctions on Iraq.

- *The need to threaten or use force occasionally to preserve access for UN weapons inspectors entails a political cost that undermines America's ability to continue containing Iraq.* Moreover, there are risks to threatening or using force. Threats that are not backed up by action undercut U.S. credibility, limited actions make the United States look feeble, and actions that fail to achieve their objective raise questions about the limits of American power. In addition, these threats cast the United States in the role of bully in the eyes of many in the Arab world and elsewhere and make it unpopular in the region.

- *While the no-drive and no-fly zones remain intact, the high operational tempo experienced by U.S. Navy and Air Force pilots and support personnel has strained operational readiness, harmed morale, and may have had an indirect impact on retention rates among pilots and others.* Moreover, the U.S. presence in the Gulf has a destabilizing impact on America's Gulf partners, and because they help defray the costs of the American presence, it is a significant financial burden for them at a time of fiscal belt-tightening.

- *America's military freedom of action has gradually diminished* as a result of a growing perception that military action cannot eliminate Iraq's WMD capabilities; that it would not succeed in compelling Iraq to cease obstructing UN weapons inspectors—and might even lead Iraq to expel UNSCOM inspectors; and that it could produce an undesirable political backlash in the Arab world and complicate relations with France, Russia, and China. The states whose support is most critical to military action—Saudi Arabia, Turkey, and Jordan—have become increasingly reluctant to permit U.S. combat aircraft to launch from their territory, fearing that doing so would expose them to domestic and regional political backlash while yielding few if any tangible strategic benefits vis-à-vis Iraq. Such flagging support for military action greatly limits America's military options and has forced the United States to rely increasingly on carrier air power, thus putting additional strains on the navy. In addition, some in Washington fear that an unsuccessful military operation would highlight the limits of American power and increase international pressure for a diplomatic solution that could compromise vital U.S. interests.

- *Broad containment is a high-maintenance policy that requires the constant care and attention of policymakers.* Senior U.S. officials have not always been able to provide containment with the degree of attention required—though this is not a problem for Saddam Husayn, for whom removing the shackles the policy places on him is a nearly all-consuming preoccupation. This has sometimes allowed Iraq to score gains without a U.S. response. And because containment is a largely reactive policy, it allows Saddam to maintain the initiative and chose the optimal time and place to challenge the international community. Moreover, keeping containment alive will, in the future, require even greater attention, resources, and concessions by the United States.

• *Few countries are willing to do what it takes to implement the policy of broad containment—in terms of intrusive inspections, sanctions, and the use of force—on an indefinite basis,* although there is widespread international support *in principle* for the policy. Moreover, some—such as France, Russia, and China, and some of the Gulf states—are edging toward an accomodationist approach. As a result, it has become increasingly difficult to implement broad containment, and efforts to do so have contributed to tensions with allies and other key states.

CONCLUSIONS

Although broad containment has many shortcomings and is increasingly difficult to sustain, it is the only policy option that stands a chance of achieving certain minimal U.S. objectives—preventing Iraq from menacing its neighbors, rebuilding its military capabilities, and threatening vital U.S. interests—without great risk or cost. If the United States stands fast in supporting UN weapons inspections and efforts to deny Iraq its oil income, and if it remains ready to use force if necessary, broad containment can continue to serve U.S. interests for at least a few more years. Clearly, however, the United States has to consider what to do after broad containment is no longer a viable policy, as a result of the collapse of the weapons inspections or sanctions regimes, at some future date.

Chapter 2

CONTAIN NARROWLY
Looking Beyond the Security Council

Kenneth M. Pollack

As distinct from the current "broad" containment of Iraq, a "narrow" containment regime would rely less on the United Nations and more on a smaller coalition of states determined to prevent Iraq from regaining its pre–Gulf War position. Narrow containment sacrifices the comprehensiveness of the current containment regime for the sake of greater sustainability, but it does not jettison all constraints on Iraq. Rather, it would seek to continue to impose the most binding restrictions on Iraqi trouble-making with or without United Nations support.

The fundamental assumption of this policy is that the current broad containment regime is unlikely to last much longer. This regime has served U.S. interests extremely well over the last seven years, but beginning with Iraq's acceptance of UN Security Council Resolution 986 in 1996, it has come under increasing strain. The most recent crisis with Iraq demonstrated the extent of political differences within the Gulf War coalition, the increasing impact of sanctions fatigue on many governments (especially in the Middle East), growing international sympathy for the plight of the Iraqi people (however exaggerated by Iraqi propoganda), and a degradation of both the inspections and sanctions regimes as a result of Resolution 1153 and the 1998 memorandum of understanding (MOU) between UN secretary general Kofi Annan and the Iraqi government.

Indeed, this policy option is largely a recognition of current realities. The United States is already being forced to make concessions in some areas of the containment regime to hold the line on others. The United States sponsored Resolution 986 to prevent the collapse of economic sanctions, and it accepted the 1998 MOU to preclude a more damaging blow to the inspections regime. As a policy option, narrow containment argues that rather than try to fight the current state of affairs, the United States would do best to accept it as an unfortunate reality and work to steer the process toward a revised containment policy, one less vulnerable to Iraqi machinations and less susceptible to the caprices of the Security Council.

Narrow containment thus represents a fall-back position from broad containment. Yet, the United States cannot assume that it can quickly switch to this policy after broad containment has fallen apart. That will be too late. The government will need months, if not years, to put in place a narrow containment regime. In particular, the United States will be able to secure many of the most important pieces of narrow containment only by agreeing now to sacrifice elements of broad containment—elements that will be the first to go when the current containment regime begins to crumble. The danger is that if the United States does not shift to narrow containment soon, it will be unable to implement the policy when broad containment unravels in the near future, because it will have lost the time and leverage it now enjoys. At that point, the administration will have no choice but to opt for one of the more dangerous alternatives of deterrence or rollback.

GOALS

The goals of a policy of narrow containment are to prevent Saddam Husayn's Iraq from making mischief beyond its borders and to limit the forces the Iraqi dictator would have for aggression. To this end, narrow containment seeks to limit Iraq's ability to rebuild its conventional forces and to prevent Iraq from rebuilding an offensive military capability. It similarly seeks to hinder (if not prevent) Iraq from reacquiring an arsenal of weapons of mass destruction (WMD) that could be used to pressure or compel other Middle Eastern states to comply with Iraq's wishes. It seeks to limit Iraq's diplomatic clout and to block any Iraqi diplomatic, military, or other efforts to influence events in the Middle East. Finally it emphasizes continued monitoring of the Iraqi economy, to keep Baghdad isolated and help ensure that Saddam is unable to rebuild his conventional or WMD arsenals.

Narrow containment is not intended to *cause* the collapse of Saddam Husayn's regime—only to prevent it from destabilizing the Gulf. It is not designed to bring about Saddam's overthrow. To the extent that it does try to exert pressure on Saddam (pressure that could, theoretically, lead to his overthrow) it does so to limit his freedom of action.

DESCRIPTION OF THE POLICY

To move from the current broad containment regime toward a narrow containment regime, three steps are required.

- The United States will have to identify key regional and extraregional states willing to participate in a coalition to implement narrow containment of Iraq, if necessary without the backing of the UN Security Council.
- The United States, in consultation with its partners in the new coalition, will have to determine the minimal requirements for containing Iraq, the elements of the current containment regime for which ongoing support is likely, and those elements that may have to be sacrificed to ensure that Washington can obtain its minimal requirements.
- Washington will have to lay the diplomatic and military groundwork for enforcement mechanisms.

The model Washington should follow is America's containment of North Korea since 1953. During the Korean War, the United States was able to act under the auspices of the United Nations—which, as in the Gulf War, was extremely useful at the time. Yet, this changed when the USSR returned to the UN Security Council: As in the case of Iraq today, the UN increasingly became a hindrance rather than a help in containing the Pyongyang regime.[1] Consequently, America built a smaller coalition of states—essentially just South Korea and Japan—fully committed to containing North Korea and willing to take all necessary measures to do so. Narrow containment of North Korea has worked extremely well. It has greatly reduced Pyongyang's ability to make mischief in East Asia for forty-five years. Thus, by sacrificing the potency of the broad containment of North Korea (i.e., the UN-based effort that existed until the return of the USSR to the Security Council), the United States was able to build a narrow containment regime that has succeeded over the long-term.

Building a New Coalition

The first step for the United States will be to create a new coalition of states willing to participate in a narrow containment regime. Membership in this group should be determined only by a state's willingness both to act to contain Iraq in the absence of a Security Council imprimatur, and to support all measures—including the use of force—to contain Iraq. These states need not be willing to employ force themselves; their willingness to do so would be desirable, but the United States should be prepared to be the sole executor of military action against Iraq and should seek only firm support from its coalition partners.

Moreover, it is not sufficient for a state to oppose Iraqi aggression, repression, or development of weapons of mass destruction for inclusion in the coalition. Many states in the world fall into this category, but few are willing to support the actions (especially the use of force) often required to make a containment regime effective. Indeed, this is the central problem of the current broad containment regime: too many states that recognize the danger Saddam's regime poses but are unwilling to take the hard actions necessary to keep the regime contained.

There is only one country whose full participation in a new anti-Iraq coalition is absolutely essential: Kuwait. As long as the United States can rely on full Kuwaiti support to allow U.S. military forces to strike Iraq whenever necessary, a policy of narrow containment is viable. (Saudi Arabia, Jordan, or Turkey could also play this role, but none has demonstrated a willingness to do so. To date, only Kuwait has provided the United States with full support for military operations against Iraq.) To ensure continued Kuwaiti support, the United States must assure Kuwait that Washington will not abandon it under any circumstances. This may require that the U.S. military augment its ground and air forces in Kuwait—for example by increasing its on-hand strength at Camp Doha from a battalion to a brigade or by adding a composite air wing to the squadron of A-10s normally based there.

Including Saudi Arabia, Jordan, and Turkey in a new coalition is not as vital as including Kuwait, but it would be *extremely* beneficial. Their participation would ensure increased cooperation in stemming the flow of proscribed goods to Iraq. It would limit Saddam's freedom of action in Middle East diplomacy. It would provide the United States with additional bases in the region—bases closer than Kuwait to targets in northern and western Iraq—and greater flexibility in developing strike missions against Iraqi targets. Saudi Arabia could also help defray the costs of the containment regime, although Saudi participation would be important more for diplomatic and military than for financial reasons. Nevertheless, even if these countries were unwilling to participate in a new coalition, the United States should assure them that its commitment to their defense—especially against an attack by Iraq—remains unequivocal.

To the extent that other Middle Eastern states could be brought into the coalition, this too would be very desirable, albeit not crucial. Bahrain and Oman appear to be reasonable candidates based on past actions. Yet, they may be wary of getting out ahead of the Saudis should Riyadh react coolly to the new policy. On the other hand, the United Arab Emirates (UAE) and Qatar appear increasingly antipathetic to the continued containment of Iraq. Similarly, it seems unlikely that Egypt could be brought on board, although doing so would be a major coup because of Cairo's diplomatic influence in the Arab world.

Beyond the states of the region, the United States should be very careful in its choice of coalition partners. Britain and Japan have demonstrated staunch support for containing Saddam and they have been the only two U.S. allies to back U.S. military reprisals against Iraq with any consistency. They are naturals. Certain other European, South American, and Asian states—the Netherlands, Argentina, and perhaps South Korea—that have also endorsed a tough line against Iraq might also be brought into the coalition. *But the United States must be adamant in favoring a smaller coalition of states with complete commitment to an assertive containment regime, rather than a larger coalition of states that will support only a weak containment regime.*

What to Preserve

Although Iraq will have to be contained by a smaller coalition of nations than currently does the job, the United States and its partners would continue to seek international agreements to hold Iraq in check, where possible. The key will be to identify those measures that are both critical to containing Iraqi aggression over the long-term and acceptable to the international community.

By showing a willingness to compromise on major elements of the current broad containment policy before it falls apart, the United States and its coalition partners will have considerable leverage to bolster those elements of the current policy that must be preserved to prevent Iraq from again destabilizing the region. Indeed, many countries—even those, like France, that want an end to the sanctions—recognize that Iraq will have to be restricted indefinitely in certain areas to prevent it from once again becoming a threat to regional peace. Therefore, the United States and its coalition partners should be able to get international agreement to continue (or restructure) many of the most important constraints on Iraq.

Rather than proposing direct tradeoffs ("if you agree to keep this element, we the United States will give up that element"), the United States should decide which parts of the current containment strategy are essential and then consider what could be sacrificed if necessary. The United States must maintain three components of the current containment regime—to begin with the essential items—if it is to keep Saddam sufficiently weak and limit his freedom of action outside Iraq. First, Washington must greatly constrain, if not prevent, Iraq from rebuilding its conventional forces. Second, it cannot allow Iraq to rebuild weapons of mass destruction. Third, Washington must limit Saddam Husayn's diplomatic "clout" and ensure that Iraq continues to be treated as a pariah state. A fourth element—closely monitoring, and if possible controlling, the Iraqi economy— would be very useful, but it is not critical.

The coalition must also realize that it may not be able to convince the Security Council to contain Saddam beyond the current sanctions regime. The coalition will then need to do whatever it takes to maintain the essential elements of the narrow containment regime. In the event the Security Council balks on certain issues, the coalition will need to take unilateral steps to substitute for those measures that the Security Council is unwilling to accept.

Limiting Iraqi Conventional Military Capabilities

Iraq's ability to destabilize the Gulf region depends primarily on its conventional military strength. The greatest source of Iraqi influence in the region has traditionally been its conventional military power. Iraq has provoked wars or crises with Iran, Kuwait, Saudi Arabia, Jordan, and Syria only when it has felt confident of its conventional military superiority. Saddam chose to defy the U.S.-led coalition during the Gulf War because he mistakenly believed his conventional strength could stalemate the coalition. Moreover, conventional military operations have been Iraq's preferred method of imposing its foreign policy designs on the rest of the region. Whenever Baghdad has been unable to get its way by dint of (usually quite incompetent) diplomacy, it has not hesitated to use force or the threat of force. If the United States is to keep Saddam's regime contained, Iraq's conventional military capabilities, and particularly its ability to project power beyond its borders, must be limited. Three complementary approaches could be used to this end.

1. *The United States and its coalition partners could seek a Security Council resolution banning the sale of "offensive" weapons to Iraq.* Specifically, the resolution would forbid the sale to Iraq of any armored combat vehicles, armed helicopters, artillery greater than 100 mm, combat aircraft, or warships in excess of 1,000 tons. It should also have provisions to allow all other member states to apply automatic sanctions on any state violating the resolution.

The controls on Iraqi imports could also be extended and toughened. At present, a UN committee scrutinizes Iraqi import agreements to ensure that they consist of only food, medicine, and other humanitarian supplies. This system could be maintained even beyond the lifting of the economic embargo to ensure that Iraq is unable to rebuild its arsenals. Alternatively, once the economic embargo is lifted, the UN could continue to monitor Iraqi imports to block the transfer of offensive conventional weapons, WMDs, and dual-use technology that Iraq could use to resuscitate its indigenous WMD capabilities. Opposition to such measures may be surmountable. Even most of Iraq's staunchest advocates, including France and Russia, recognize that a rearmed Iraq will likely return to its past patterns of aggression. Their paramount concern is to see an end to the economic embargo so they can profit from the sale of Iraqi oil, but they have no particular desire to allow Iraq to reemerge as a source of instability in the Gulf. Indeed, many of their diplomats have privately expressed a desire to see Iraqi military forces limited even well after the economic sanctions have been lifted. Of course, some states—primarily China—may claim that Iraq should be allowed to rebuild its conventional forces to meet "legitimate defense requirements," but given Iraq's history of aggression and the pledge Saddam will be required to give that Iraq will not attack any of its neighbors (see below), it may be possible to convince even the Chinese that Iraq can meet its *defense* needs without any of the banned weapons systems.

2. *Especially if the Security Council refuses to act, the coalition could establish an international regime for Iraq similar to the Cold War's Coordinating Committee for Multilateral Export Controls (COCOM), which would prohibit the sale or transfer of any weapons or sophisticated technology.* The coalition could exert all possible diplomatic pressure to convince other states, especially the European Union, not to sell weaponry to Iraq. The coalition could announce a joint agreement to impose harsh sanctions against any nation that does provide such arms to Iraq.

3. *Another way to handle the issue of Iraqi conventional forces that could prove suitable to coalition objectives would be to create a conventional arms control regime for the Gulf similar to the Conventional Forces in Europe (CFE) regime established in western and eastern Europe at the end of the Cold War.* In return for drastic limits on Iraqi conventional forces, the United States and its coalition partners might choose to press for similar (albeit much more generous) restrictions on Iranian,

Gulf Cooperation Council (GCC), and even American forces in the region. Such an agreement would have to contain provisions for the monitoring and inspection of all forces in the region to make it effective, again probably along the lines of the CFE treaty. Although this course would be very difficult to realize in practice, if achieved, it not only would create a powerful mechanism to prevent Iraq from destabilizing the Gulf, but also could keep other regional states from doing the same.

Denying Iraq Weapons of Mass Destruction

A close second to preventing Iraq from reconstituting its conventional forces is preventing it from rebuilding its WMD and ballistic missile arsenal. In the past, Saddam has employed these forces against Israel, Iran, Saudi Arabia, and Bahrain. They are an important source of Iraqi regional prestige, they have proven a helpful asset in his conventional military campaigns, and they have deterred other states from standing up to Iraq. Moreover, if Saddam were ever to obtain a deliverable nuclear weapons capability, he would likely use the leverage it would provide him to pursue his regional ambitions. Consequently, even though WMDs cannot conquer other countries and are often a poor instrument of diplomacy, it would be very dangerous to allow Saddam to rebuild his WMD arsenal.

To prevent this, the United States and its coalition partners should seek a new Security Council resolution reaffirming the sections of Resolution 687 that forbid Iraq from again rebuilding its arsenal of weapons of mass destruction—even as a purely defensive measure. This resolution should not provide for specific consequences should Iraq violate it, but should instead state that any Iraqi violation will be treated under Chapter VII of the UN charter as a threat to the national security of all member states. In addition, the coalition should demand a public statement by Saddam Husayn reaffirming Iraq's commitment to cooperate in perpetuity with the long-term monitoring regime of the UN Special Committee on Iraq (UNSCOM) and pledging to rebuild neither Iraq's weapons of mass destruction nor its ballistic missiles. Given that there is complete unanimity among the international community that Iraq should not be allowed to rebuild its WMD force, these measures may arouse few complaints. Baghdad will have a very tough time explaining why it should not reaffirm what it has already been forced to accept and repeatedly follow. A provision more likely to arouse opposition is the demand for Iraqi violations to be treated under Chapter VII of the UN charter, because Iraq and some of its advocates may view it as constituting preapproval for U.S. military reprisals against Iraq. Consequently, the United States and its coalition partners may have to make concessions on the current sanctions regime to secure this measure.

Limiting Iraq's Diplomatic and Military Freedom of Action

The last critical element of continued containment of Iraq is to ensure that Baghdad has little influence in the Gulf, the Middle East, or anywhere else in the world. Saddam has repeatedly demonstrated that he views any relationship or any status Iraq may have as levers to be manipulated in pursuit of his regional ambitions. With the lifting of economic sanctions it will be impossible to keep Iraq completely isolated: Oil exports and imports of everything from food to manufactured goods will once again give Iraq significant economic standing. Yet, the coalition must do what it can to constrain Saddam's ability to employ that clout.

In particular, the coalition must make clear that it would respond if Iraq ever employed force beyond its borders. Obviously, the prohibition on the sale of offensive weapons to Iraq will be the most important element of this effort, but the coalition should take further steps to preclude a return to Saddam's past belligerence. The coalition should persuade the Security

Council to pass a new resolution reaffirming the sections of Resolution 687 that guarantee the international borders of Kuwait. Moreover, the coalition should require Saddam himself to make a public statement reaffirming the sovereignty of Kuwait and the inviolability of its borders and promising that Iraq will never again use force beyond its borders, under any circumstances.

By assuring regional states that Iraq has been forbidden from using force beyond its borders, by denying it the wherewithal to do so, and by making clear that the United States and its coalition partners have the strength and political will to enforce these restrictions (see below), Iraq's ability to influence its neighbors will be greatly diminished. Moreover, the mere fact that these restrictions exist and are meticulously enforced by the world's only remaining superpower and its coalition partners will be a constant reminder to the rest of the world that Saddam Husayn's Iraq is not, and will never be, fully accepted back into the community of nations.

For these same reasons it is important that, in negotiating the lifting of sanctions, the focus of U.S. diplomatic efforts should not be Iraq, but the rest of the international community and particularly Iraq's most important advocates: France, Russia, and China. The United States and its coalition partners should not negotiate with Saddam, nor should they make tradeoffs designed to convince *him* to compromise. Instead, Washington should negotiate only with the French, Russians, and Chinese acting as Iraq's advocates and make tradeoffs to get *them* to compromise. It is important that Saddam be denied the prestige of negotiating with the United States. Moreover, the French, Russians, and Chinese have much more modest goals than does Saddam. For instance, they are all generally interested in depriving Iraq of its WMD arsenal, whereas Saddam clearly is not. Consequently, striking bargains with them will be much easier and more useful than striking bargains with Saddam.

Monitoring the Iraqi Economy

The policy of narrow containment assumes that the United States and its coalition allies will be unable to prevent the eventual lifting of the economic sanctions on Iraq. Yet, it is reasonable to believe that the coalition may be able to continue to monitor the Iraqi economy and perhaps control certain elements of Iraqi spending to ensure that Baghdad is unable to cheat on the remaining restrictions on its military and diplomatic activities.

The best way to keep an eye on how Saddam Husayn is spending Iraq's money is to secure passage of the UN Security Council resolutions described above that would retain the UN escrow account and monitoring committee (established by Resolution 661) to oversee Iraqi expenditures and ensure that Iraq is unable to purchase offensive conventional weapons, WMDs, or dual-use technology. Yet, additional methods are also available. For instance, the coalition could insist that Iraq comply with Resolution 687's stipulation that Baghdad pay a percentage of its oil revenues as compensation for the losses sustained by the victims of its aggression. This serves two useful purposes: First, it takes roughly 30 percent of Iraqi oil revenues out of Saddam's hands and gives them to his victims. Second, it keeps in place UN monitoring of the Iraqi oil industry. Such monitoring allows the international community to have a sense of how much money Baghdad has available to it (thereby making it easier to supervise Iraqi imports) and ensures that large numbers of international personnel are in Iraq keeping tabs on Saddam's regime.

Forcing Iraq to continue to pay compensation could serve several other functions as well. To the extent that countries such as France and Russia object that forcing Iraq to pay compensation makes it impossible for Baghdad to repay them for pre–Gulf War debts, the compensation itself could be used for debt repayment. The coalition could agree to allow the UN to repay valid loans from member countries made to Iraq prior to the invasion of Kuwait. Likewise, the oil Iraq sells to Jordan at a discount could be brought under UN control and made part of Iraq's compensation package.

Although these various economic measures are not critical to the success of a narrow containment regime, they would be very useful complements to the vital military and diplomatic constraints on Iraq. The coalition should be loath to bargain them away except in return for very considerable concessions from the other side. At the very least, some form of continuing economic restrictions should be employed temporarily, as part of a gradual process of the lifting of sanctions to ensure Baghdad's good behavior. Nevertheless, the United States and its coalition partners should not make holding on to these aspects of the current containment regime a limiting factor on its own freedom of action. A critical element of narrow containment is limiting the extent to which the coalition must rely on the Security Council: If the only way to get these various economic restrictions enacted would be to again surrender the coalition's freedom of action to the Security Council, the coalition should pass on the deal.

Tradeoffs to Ensure Containment

The next step will be for the United States and its coalition partners to determine which elements of the current UN sanctions can be sacrificed to lock-in the critical aspects of a long-term containment regime. The fundamental premise of the narrow containment policy option is that the most constraining aspects of the current sanctions regime—the economic embargo and the ban on Iraqi oil sales—cannot be sustained for much longer. Indeed, Resolution 1153 has effectively lifted the ban on Iraqi oil sales, leaving in place only the economic embargo and UN control of Iraqi purchases under Resolution 986. Nevertheless, it is equally clear that if the United States were willing, it could sustain these measures probably for several years or longer (see the previous chapter on broad containment) even in the face of Iraqi, French, Russian, and Chinese pressures. Thus, both Baghdad and its diplomatic advocates should be willing to make considerable concessions to see an early end to the economic embargo.

Determining which elements of the current sanctions regime should be sacrificed can occur only as part of the negotiating process itself. The requirements listed above constitute the most desirable aspects of a narrow containment regime, and the United States and its coalition partners should be willing to make considerable tradeoffs to secure them. But clearly, if the coalition is unable to attain its goals, then it should not be willing to compromise as quickly or as deeply on its own end. The tradeoffs described below, therefore, reflect the maximum sacrifices the coalition should be willing to make in return for full agreement with its demands. Lesser compromises by those representing Iraq should be met only with lesser concessions from the coalition.

The most important concession the United States and its coalition partners could make would be to end the economic embargo on Iraq. Because of the stipulations of the various UN Security Council resolutions, this could not be done arbitrarily, but the coalition could take at least two major steps to aid this process. First, it could agree to accept the strict interpretation of paragraph 22 of Resolution 687, which would relinquish UN control of Iraqi oil sales (and therefore most restrictions on Iraqi imports) after UNSCOM has certified the destruction of Iraq's WMD programs and has transitioned from inspecting to long-term monitoring. Second, it could agree to a timetable for lifting the economic sanctions—something Iraq has been requesting for several years. Indeed, in return for support for their position, the coalition members should even be willing to agree to a fairly rapid timetable for the lifting of economic sanctions.

There are other aspects of the current sanctions regime which could likewise be traded for new measures to help contain Iraq. For example, UN resolutions require Iraq to pay compensation for the losses sustained by the victims of its aggression; they impose a ban on all flights to and from Iraq; they have frozen Iraqi assets overseas; they demand that Iraq return equipment stolen from Kuwait since the invasion; and they demand that Baghdad repatriate the Kuwaiti citizens deported to Iraq during the Iraqi occupation. Moreover, the United States and other member states have taken certain actions under the auspices of the UN, albeit without the authorization of a specific resolution. The most important of these is their imposition of the no-fly zones over southern and northern Iraq and the no-drive zone in the South. Compromises could be made on each of these points. Compensation could be scaled back and a time limit placed on payments; Iraq's assets could be unfrozen; the flight ban lifted; nonmilitary equipment stolen from Kuwait forgotten; and other issues set aside. Similarly, both no-fly zones and the no-drive zone could be terminated—which would also prove a relief to the U.S. Air Force.

Also, the United States and its coalition partners could consider compromising on the standard of compliance with the initial UNSCOM inspections. UNSCOM and the IAEA appear confident that they have a good handle on Iraq's nuclear and ballistic missile programs. The time may not be far off when UNSCOM decides that it can cease the inspection process and transition to long-term monitoring in these two areas. Yet, it seems highly unlikely that UNSCOM will ever be entirely satisfied that the Iraqis have eliminated their chemical and biological warfare (CW and BW) arsenals. Moreover, at some point in the next few years, the international community probably will become reluctant to continue delaying the lifting of sanctions if UNSCOM can account for all but 5 percent or 10 percent of the CW and BW materials it believes

Iraq manufactured. The United States and its coalition partners should be willing to consider relaxing somewhat the standards on Iraqi compliance with the UNSCOM inspections if doing so would allow them to lock-in other, more important constraints over the long term.

Finally, the United States could make sacrifices on other foreign policy issues in return for cooperation from other states in containing Iraq. Washington must explicitly acknowledge that, at present, Iraq is arguably America's single greatest foreign policy concern in the Middle East. Of all the difficulties in the Middle East, only Saddam Husayn currently has the real potential to cause major damage to U.S. interests both regionally and globally. On the other hand, few other states are as concerned with the future of Iraq as they are with other foreign issues. If the United States is willing to make concessions on those issues that matter most to other countries, it is likely that they will be willing to make concessions on Iraq. A prime example of this is Iran. Most European states are far more interested in rehabilitating Iran than rehabilitating Iraq. Especially in light of the real changes President Muhammad Khatemi is introducing in Iran, the United States should be willing to negotiate a reduction in the U.S. sanctions on Iran in return for European acceptance of some of the more far-reaching measures suggested above. Indeed, such a policy might also have the added benefit of securing further Iranian cooperation in the containment of Iraq. Other examples might include increasing U.S. military assistance to Egypt and Jordan, acceding to the proposals of the UAE in the negotiations on legal jurisdiction over U.S. military personnel on leave in Dubai, and minimizing congressional interference in arms sales to Turkey.

Enforcing the Agreement

A narrow containment regime will see less use of force against Iraq. In fact, because the restrictions on Iraq will be greatly reduced from the current broad containment regime, the Iraqis will probably run up against the restrictions of a narrow containment regime less frequently than under broad containment. Moreover, once Saddam is convinced that the United States and its coalition allies have the political will to use force to support the remaining elements of narrow containment, he will probably be more wary of provoking a military response; the absence of Security Council shackles on the coalition will allow the United States to retaliate far more forcefully than under broad containment. The key is to make sure Saddam believes that the coalition has the will to enforce the containment regime and that it will make him pay a very heavy price for challenging it.

Therefore, on those occasions when the coalition deems it necessary to use military force against Iraq, the blows should be disproportionate to the provocation and executed in anger rather than sorrow. The nature of the response—air strikes, cruise missiles, commando-type raids, ground incursions, and so forth—is unimportant. Of paramount importance are the targets struck, the amount of damage done, the speed of the response, and the amount of pressure applied.

Military reprisals should be directed at targets designed to inflict maximum pain on Saddam Husayn. Because the role of the Security Council will be negligible under such a regime, Washington should not feel compelled to make its response proportionate or relevant to the Iraqi provocation. Indeed, because this containment regime will operate in the absence of international consensus, it will be crucial to demonstrate to Saddam that even without UN dispensation, the coalition can make Iraq pay a heavy price for misbehavior. Thus, the coalition should target that which Saddam values most: the Special Republican Guard, the Republican Guard, the Iraqi Air Force, Iraq's internal security forces, and other high-value military targets (like its free-rocket-over-ground [FROG] rocket launchers).

The amount of damage inflicted must be visibly significant: It is crucial to send an unmistakable message to Saddam that the coalition is serious about punishing him for malfeasance. The reprisal should come very quickly after the Iraqi provocation. If Saddam believes he will have a period of time between an Iraqi action and a coalition reaction he may conclude either that this will allow him to employ that window to his advantage or that he could use that time to bring diplomatic pressure to bear on the United States to preclude the retaliation. Saddam can have no illusion that he may be able to establish a *fait accompli*; the coalition must retaliate against his transgressions immediately to convince him that he can gain nothing from further provocations.

The coalition must be prepared to conduct sustained military operations against Iraq. Although Saddam has proven sensitive to U.S. military strikes over the last seven years, this may not always be true in the future. The coalition must be prepared to exert more military pressure on Saddam than he is willing to absorb—which could require days or even weeks of military operations.

The coalition must also have an unequivocal commitment to the aggressive use of force against Iraq, especially early on. Saddam will no doubt see the end of the UN-led containment regime as a victory and will attempt to exploit it. In addition, he will seek to test the determination of the new coalition. Meanwhile, with the UN sanctions largely gone, the coalition will have far fewer options available—other than the use of force—to punish Saddam for his transgressions. Consequently, it is imperative that the United States—with the vocal support and possibly the participation of its coalition partners—employ force in response to Iraqi provocations to demonstrate to Saddam that the coalition has the political will to keep him down even without the blessing of the Security Council. It will be equally important to demonstrate to the rest of the world the seriousness with which the coalition views the continued containment of Iraq, to dissuade other countries from cooperating with Iraq in arms smuggling and other illicit activities.

END STATE

The goal of the policy of narrow containment is to prevent Saddam Husayn from making mischief beyond Iraq's borders until the internal contradictions inherent in his regime bring about its collapse—or until he dies in his bed. Containment *per se* is not concerned with bringing about any particular end state. Instead it is a defensive strategy that simply seeks to prevent Iraq from doing harm until other forces prompt a change in the regime.

Nevertheless, this should not prevent the coalition from articulating a set of conditions under which they should consider narrow containment to have "succeeded" and therefore bring it to an end. Among these conditions are the following:

- Saddam Husayn must no longer rule—even indirectly—in Baghdad. Saddam's unique combination of ambitions and pathologies make him personally too dangerous to regional stability for containment to be discontinued while he is in power.
- A successor regime must demonstrate a total commitment to the Nuclear Non-Proliferation Treaty (NPT), the Biological Weapons Convention (BWC), and the Chemical Weapons Convention (CWC) so that other regional states can feel secure that Iraq's WMD programs will conform to international norms and be under international monitoring.
- A successor regime must also renounce all Iraqi land claims beyond its international borders and must in particular recognize Kuwaiti sovereignty and its international borders.
- A successor regime must further agree to limit its conventional military establishment to a purely defensive force. No effort should be made to define what constitutes a "purely

defensive force"—the coalition (not Iraq) should retain the prerogative to determine that based on circumstances.

ADVANTAGES

A policy of narrow containment would offer Washington several advantages. Among them, it would do the following:

- *Allow the United States to continue to pursue a policy of containing Iraq over the long term.* Containment has the advantage of avoiding the much greater costs and risks associated with nearly every other option.
- *Allow for greater flexibility within the policy than the current containment regime.* Narrow containment allows for the sacrifice of those elements of the current containment regime that are unsustainable over the long term. It focuses U.S. efforts on only those elements of the regime truly necessary to constrain Iraqi aggression.
- *Greatly minimize the ability of Russia, China, and other states to undermine U.S. containment of Iraq.* Because the UN Security Council will not be asked to support the narrow coalition's actions, there will be less occasion to expose and amplify differences between the United States and other council members, such as Russia and China.
- *Undermine Iraqi propaganda attacks that containment causes human suffering among the Iraqi people.*

LIABILITIES AND RISKS

Along with the advantages listed above, a policy of narrow containment of Iraq would have certain negative characteristics; it would, for example, do the following:

- *Sacrifice a very strong containment regime for a weaker one.* The current UN-based containment regime is the strongest the world has ever seen and puts tremendous pressure on Saddam Husayn. The proposed narrow containment regime would not be as strong, nor would it put the same kind of pressure on Saddam.

- *Incur the risk that, once the United States starts retreating on aspects of the sanctions regime, it will not be able to stop.* Iraq will play up a shift in U.S. policy as a great defeat for Washington. It may require considerable diplomatic and public relations efforts to convince other nations that a move to narrow containment is not merely a fig leaf to cover the collapse of U.S. policy toward Iraq.

- *Require considerable diplomatic and public relations exertions to convince other nations to accept some of the more far-reaching elements of the proposed containment regime.* This is especially so given the fact that Washington will have "momentum" against it. Thus the transition will have to be handled carefully to dispel any appearance of a U.S. rout.

- *Require the United States to employ military force to block Iraqi provocations.* Without the UN sanctions, the burden of preventing Iraqi aggression and punishing it for other provocations (such as tampering with UNSCOM's long-term monitoring regime) will fall entirely on the United States and our willingness to use force to compel Saddam.

- *Not be a quick fix policy.* Containment is inherently unpalatable to many people because it is a purely defensive policy. Containment seeks to prevent Iraq from destabilizing the Gulf region until Saddam Husayn falls. It does not include any mechanism to cause him to fall. Consequently, it cannot promise an end to the problem of Saddam Husayn in the near term. The United States must expect to contain Iraq for many more years, if not decades, as has been the case for North Korea.

- *Make no provisions for who will succeed Saddam.* As a purely defensive strategy, containment will limit the ability of the United States to influence the post-Saddam government.

- *Risk that Iraq reconstitutes its conventional and*

nonconventional weapons capability. The North Korean case is instructive: Pyongyang was never able to build a first-class conventional military, but it did rebuild enough conventional military power to be able to threaten the South with tremendous destruction in the event of a war. Moreover, although it took forty years, North Korea was able to build a nuclear weapons capability. (It should be noted that North Korea had something Iraq will not: two friendly great power neighbors that shared a land border with it and that were willing to provide it with arms and dual-use technology. The coalition should find it much easier to prevent such transfers to Iraq than was the case for North Korea, because of the difference in their geopolitical positions.)

- *Highlight the U.S. relationship with Kuwait, which could be problematic.* First, it might require Kuwait to take a more independent course than the rest of the GCC, something it has tried to avoid in the past. Second, the U.S. public may be reluctant to spend so much for a policy designed to defend authoritarian Kuwait. (On the other hand, South Korea was hardly a model democracy in 1953. Moreover, because of the close involvement of the United States, South Korea has developed into a democracy and—although it has a long way to go—for the same reason Kuwait too has made the most progress toward democracy of any of the Gulf states.)

Narrow containment has one final disadvantage: *The Republicans have made clear that they oppose continued containment of Iraq and instead want a more proactive policy to actually oust Saddam.*

CONCLUSIONS

Narrow containment is a way of minimizing Iraq's ability to threaten its neighbors and to destabilize the Gulf region without the risks and costs associated with policies such as deter-

Iraq Strategy Review   57

rence or some variation of rollback. Nevertheless, it has very serious drawbacks: It cannot promise to bring about an end to Saddam Husayn's regime, nor does it exert as much pressure on Baghdad as does the current broad containment regime. Consequently, it is a policy to be employed if and when the United States is unwilling both to pay the costs required to remove Saddam's regime and to run the risk of giving Saddam the kind of freedom he would enjoy if containment were abandoned in favor of deterrence. Moreover, the critical assumption of narrow containment is that broad containment is unsustainable over the long term. If broad containment can be sustained, then it is clearly preferable to narrow containment. Yet, if the U.S. government concludes that the pressure on the current containment policy does threaten its collapse in the next few years, then narrow containment offers a highly attractive alternative to the more extreme options.

NOTE

[1]   In January 1950, in a bid to have the United Nations recognize Peking (Beijing) rather than Taipei as the legitimate Chinese government and grant the People's Republic of China a seat on the Security Council, the USSR boycotted the United Nations. The impact of this decision was felt most strongly on June 25, 1950, when North Korea invaded the Republic of Korea, and the United States requested that the Security Council—free from a potential Soviet veto—order the UN to aid South Korea militarily. The Soviet Union initially took the threat lightly but soon realized that U.S. and UN forces would not be easily expelled. Thus, the Soviet Union announced the end of its boycott on August 1, 1950. The return of the USSR weakened the "virtual unanimity" of the United Nations on the Korean question, as the Soviet Union brought with it a communist view of the conflict.

Chapter 3

UNDERMINE
Supporting the Iraqi Opposition

Daniel L. Byman and Kenneth M. Pollack

T he "Undermine" option uses the Iraqi opposition to destabilize Saddam Husayn's regime and thereby create the circumstances in which he could be overthrown. Although Saddam's removal from power is the ultimate objective of this policy, it recognizes the inherent difficulty of such a program and therefore allows for graduated support for the opposition based on demonstrated effectiveness: The more effective the opposition group, the more support it would receive.

The rationale behind a policy of undermining the Iraqi regime is to create conditions that will hasten Saddam's fall while minimizing, to the greatest extent possible, the cost and risk to the United States. Rather than simply attempting to limit Saddam's troublemaking potential (the goal of containment) or minimizing his impact on U.S. foreign policy (the goal of deterrence), undermining the regime by supporting the Iraqi opposition actually attempts to solve the problem of Saddam Husayn by fostering the circumstances that could lead to his removal. Moreover, it allows the United States to retain the initiative in the struggle with Iraq and pressure Saddam where he is most sensitive—his control over Iraq. At the same time, it holds out the prospect that the United States could rid itself of Saddam without having to incur the daunting costs inherent in an actual U.S. invasion of Iraq.

Nevertheless, because a policy directed at undermining the current regime attempts to avoid serious risk or cost to the United States, there would be no guarantee that it would succeed in ousting Saddam. Without the commitment of substan-

---

tial U.S. forces to support the opposition, a strategy for ousting Saddam would run a considerable risk (perhaps even a high likelihood) of failure (see the annex on "Overthrowing Saddam"). Ultimately, this strategy is meant to create only the *possibility* that Saddam will be overthrown, not a certainty.

This approach also holds out the prospect of achieving other, less ambitious but still useful, objectives even if it fails to spark Saddam's ouster. In particular, a modest version of overthrow could be a useful adjunct to a policy of containment by putting additional pressure on Saddam to keep him weak and compliant. Thus, even an unsuccessful policy could enjoy some success if wedded to either broad or narrow containment.

GOALS

"Undermine" has a straightforward goal: bringing about Saddam's downfall. The policy would try to accomplish this by helping the Iraqi opposition wage a guerrilla campaign against the Baghdad regime. The assumption underlying the policy is that sufficient opposition pressure on the Iraqi regime will lead to large-scale disaffection and desertions from the regime, which will create the conditions in which Saddam will be killed or overthrown.

It is conceivable, but not likely, that the opposition could itself take power. That, however, is not a necessary component of the policy. Undermine is concerned primarily with the *process* of destabilizing the regime through the instrument of the Iraqi opposition and not necessarily with the *outcome* of the process—that is to say, the makeup of a successor regime. The policy need not ensure that the Iraqi opposition will take power in the wake of Saddam's demise nor need it otherwise determine the fate of Iraq's future government. The policy assumes that "anyone but Saddam" in power in Baghdad would represent a major improvement because any successor would be less aggressive and brutal than Saddam. Although it may be preferable that the opposition take power rather than a henchman of Saddam, insisting on an opposition victory will be difficult and will make a coup or assassination less likely. If the United States wants to achieve an opposition victory, rather than just the paramount goal of removing Saddam, the cost will be much higher.

On the other hand, even if the policy did not fulfill its maximal goal of overthrowing Saddam, it could still achieve other important objectives. In particular, it could prove extremely useful in pressuring Saddam and limiting his freedom of action as part of a more aggressive policy of containment.

DESCRIPTION OF THE POLICY

A policy of undermining Saddam by supporting the Iraqi opposition faces considerable hurdles. Creating an opposition formidable enough to cause the kind of instability in Baghdad that might prompt an assassination or a coup, much less one that could actually take power, will not be easy given the current weakness of the Iraqi opposition and the strength of Saddam's grip on power. Thus, the policy would envision a five-phase insurgent strategy that, it is hoped, would end in a situation in which the central government was sufficiently weakened and demoralized that it would be vulnerable to a coup or assassination. Each phase would lay the foundation for the next, allowing the opposition to progress gradually from the least difficult to the most difficult tasks. The phases of the insurgency strategy would proceed as follows:

1. *Broaden and strengthen the opposition.* Incorporate new figures into the opposition leadership and recruit new opposition fighters. Simultaneously, augment opposition propaganda directed against the regime, to attract recruits, put pressure on the regime, and convince Saddam's henchmen to defect from his cause.

2. *Establish one or more safe-havens* either in the

Kurdish-held North or in a neighboring state, and train a guerrilla force capable of waging an insurgency against Saddam's regime.

3. *Begin hit-and-run operations into Iraq* from the safe-haven area.

4. *Move the guerrilla force into Iraq and establish an exclusion zone on Iraqi terrain,* possibly with U.S. airpower helping to defend the exclusion zone from regime forces.

5. *Expand guerrilla operations deeper and deeper into Iraq* to weaken central government control over the country, demoralize the regime, and humiliate Saddam Husayn.

Thus, the insurgent campaign would build from merely harassing the regime, to limiting the amount of territory under the regime's control, and eventually to weakening the regime's control throughout the country.

To make the opposition viable, Washington will have to provide assistance in a wide variety of areas. The United States will have to help rebuild the Iraqi opposition; secure a functional safe-haven for it; seduce Saddam's henchman to turn against the regime; provide the opposition with considerable military assistance; and run interference for it in the diplomatic arena, while simultaneously keeping Saddam tightly contained.

U.S. support could be graduated to be taken as quickly or slowly as Washington deems appropriate. At each step, the United States would have to determine whether the opposition was progressing sufficiently to warrant additional support. Nonetheless, any variant of this policy will require a fairly considerable effort on the part of the United States. There is a minimum level of support required simply to rebuild the Iraqi opposition and to give it the ability to undertake any kind of mission—even if it is never able to conduct anything more than minor harassing operations.

In judging how to proceed with a policy of undermining Saddam, historical analogies can be dangerous. Although Afghanistan is regularly cited as a precedent by advocates of this course, the Afghan model is of only limited applicability to Iraq today. Afghanistan was menaced by a brutal outside invader—the Soviet Union. Iraq's tyranny, in contrast, is entirely home-grown. Thus, the nationalistic impulse that led many Afghans to take up arms is not present in Iraq today. Furthermore, although U.S. support for the *mujahedin* did lead (eventually) to the fall of the Soviet-backed government, it did not lead to the end of the civil war. Perhaps of greatest importance, the Soviet Union could have withdrawn from Afghanistan; Saddam cannot withdraw from Iraq. Nor does Iraq fit the pattern of the successful coups engineered by the United States in the past. In the "countercoup" in Iran and coups in Guatemala, the Dominican Republic, Vietnam, and elsewhere, the United States had a wide range of contacts with local political and military leaders who formed the successor governments. Thus, diplomatic and intelligence personnel could orchestrate the coup, identifying the leaders in advance and helping them achieve their goals. In Iraq, on the other hand, the United States has few if any contacts with Saddam's inner circle.

Bolstering the Opposition

At present, the Iraqi opposition is far from ready to mount even a modest challenge to Saddam's regime. The various opposition groups are fragmented and fractious. Despite the existence of the Iraq National Congress (INC) as an umbrella organization, the Iraqi opposition is in no way united and cannot coordinate its resistance to Saddam. Part of Iraq's Kurdish opposition works with Saddam, whereas other Kurds have turned to Iran for help. Yet, despite its current weakness, the INC still offers several important advantages:
*   The INC is well-known in the West and in the United States. Many members of Congress have expressed their

support for its leadership, making it easier for the administration to gain domestic support for an "undermine" strategy led by the INC.

- The United States has worked with the INC in the past, and INC leaders are eager for U.S. support. Unlike many other anti-Saddam Iraqis, such as the various Iran-based Shi'i groups, the INC does not oppose the United States.
- Existing U.S. ties to the INC will make it difficult for Washington to turn its back on the movement for political reasons. Allies in the region and potential supporters in Iraq itself will find it difficult to believe that the United States really intends to support the opposition if it publicly abandons the INC, its former ally.

At the same time, the INC also has several serious problems:

- Since Saddam's attack on the Kurdish-held city of Irbil in 1996, the INC has been a shambles: The INC's cadres have scattered, its organization has fragmented, its leadership has been discredited, and its standing in Iraq has dramatically deteriorated. Iraq's major Kurdish factions, which represented the bulk of the INC's combat forces, have abandoned the INC and are now competing for Baghdad's favor. The INC's leadership is in exile, and the limited network it had established in the country has been shattered. As a result, the INC has almost no presence or support in Iraq today.
- The INC's military track record is poor. Although the INC claims several military victories—and faults the United States for many of its failures—in truth, it has scored few successes against the Iraqi armed forces, even in their depleted post-Gulf War condition.
- The INC has not been able to arouse any real support among the Iraqi people and armed forces. During the years it operated freely in Kurdistan (1992–1996), it was able to recruit only several hundred fighters, and few Iraqi mili-

tary officers defected to its ranks. Likewise, only a handful of small Iraqi combat units (the largest was a battalion) defected to the INC—even at the height of Iraq's domestic travails—and then, the soldiers largely deserted rather than join the INC ranks.

- Of particular importance, the INC has little or no support among Iraq's Sunni core. The past dominance of the INC by Iraqi Kurds and Shi'a has traditionally alarmed Iraq's Sunnis and led them to rally around Saddam's regime.

Given these strengths and weaknesses, the first decision necessary when contemplating a policy of undermining Saddam's regime is whether to work with the INC or to stimulate creation of a new opposition.

WORK WITH THE INC . . . Given the INC's advantages, it would be most effective to find ways to reform, reorganize, and reinvigorate the INC. The INC will be able to appeal to potential dissidents in Iraq and convince regime supporters to turn on Saddam only if the average Iraqi believes Washington is strongly committed to making the INC into an efficient force. By now, the Iraqi people have concluded that the U.S. government does not want to remove Saddam from power because Washington has committed so little to doing so. If the United States is to succeed in seeing Saddam's regime undermined, American support to the Iraqi opposition must convince Iraqis—both inside and outside the regime—that the United States really wants Saddam gone.

To reinvigorate the INC, the most important step would be to greatly expand and diversify INC membership. Although the INC is nominally an umbrella organization, it does not include many important opposition groups or important Iraqi expatriates. It is vital that the INC broaden its base to include all of the opposition groups and as many Iraqi expatriates as possible. Only in this manner will Iraqis begin to see the organization as representing a true national opposition to Saddam,

rather than simply a façade for Kurdish (or Shi'i) secession-
ists. This will likely require a major shake-up of the INC leadership to incorporate new elements, get rid of "dead wood,"
and minimize the overrepresentation of some elements of Iraqi
society. To ensure that the INC reforms itself in this manner,
the United States should make clear that one criterion Washington will use to assess the progress of the opposition (and
thus the level of funding it will receive) is the extent to which
the INC can successfully diversify its membership and appeal
to all of Iraq's ethnic, religious, and tribal groups.

... OR STIMULATE CREATION OF A NEW OPPOSITION. Building a new opposition would take more time and be more of a
gamble. In place of the INC, a new opposition political movement and army would have to be assembled, probably from
former Iraqi army personnel, Kurdish *peshmerga* (resistance
fighters), and Sunni and Shi'i tribal forces. This opposition
could recruit among the Iraqi expatriate community and work
with regional governments, such as Saudi Arabia and Kuwait,
to identify likely recruits.

U.S. support will be crucial to building any effective opposition, but this would be especially true if Washington were
to drop the INC. Credibility would be a major hurdle for the
United States. Why should Iraqis flock to the new opposition
when the INC ostensibly had America's full support but was
abandoned in the crunch? The United States would similarly
have to convince regional states that the new opposition represents a real improvement over the INC, one that justifies
having abandoned the INC. Another problem may be convincing Iraqis and Arab governments alike that the new opposition
is not simply a creature of the United States and a tool designed to return Iraq to colonial servitude.

One advantage that the United States could exploit would
be that, by forging a new Iraqi opposition, Washington could
improve the leadership of the opposition. With some exceptions,

the leaderships of the extant Iraqi opposition groups are generally ineffective, corrupt, lacking in charisma, and often penetrated by the Iraqi intelligence services. A new opposition could, conceivably, offer an improvement on this score. Creating a "kinder, gentler" opposition would be difficult but not impossible. The standard should not be an Iraqi Vaclav Havel. Rather, the United States should seek leaders who represent a relative improvement over the Ba'th regime and who are willing to show minimal respect for other elites and their communities. For example, the Nicaraguan *contras* included many former Sandinistas and Somocistas, along with a sprinkling of democratic elements. With U.S. support, though, the more democratic elements of the *contras* came to the fore and helped a democratic regime take power.

PUTTING THE OPPOSITION BACK IN BUSINESS. Regardless of which path the United States were to take, it would require a major expenditure of American resources and attention to revive a functioning Iraqi opposition. As a result of many years of neglect and mismanagement, the domestic opposition to Saddam is not seen inside Iraq as a threat to his regime. Therefore, Washington would have to help a reformed INC or a new opposition group to establish itself as a viable alternative to Saddam in the minds of Iraqis. Some of the more important U.S. efforts would include the following:

- Provide all necessary funds to the opposition to enable it to progress to the point at which it is a destabilizing factor inside Iraq. This will be a long and expensive effort, although a campaign to rid the opposition of its endemic corruption could reduce the cost and simultaneously improve its image. The United States should solicit contributions from its allies in the region, in Europe, and in East Asia, but it should be prepared to pay the entire bill if necessary.
- Fund opposition radio and television stations to make the Iraqi people aware of their existence and to help them

spread the anti-Saddam message inside Iraq.
* Encourage the opposition to establish a presence inside Iraq itself as early as possible. For the opposition to succeed, it must have a strong presence in Iraq and leaders who are credible there. Thus, long before the opposition fighters and leadership return *en masse*, the opposition will need a network of informants, recruiters, and agitators in country.
* When and if the opposition moves into Iraq and establishes exclusion zones under its control, the United States should try to free these areas from United Nations (UN) sanctions and provide sufficient aid to demonstrate that life for Iraq will be better under the opposition than under Saddam.

Establishing Safe Havens

A crucial precondition of a strategy aimed at undermining the regime is finding at least one state neighboring Iraq that is willing to serve as a safe haven where members of the opposition can broadcast propaganda, shelter their families, train, recruit, and arm. Even if the opposition progresses to the point at which it can move into Iraq and carve out chunks of Iraqi territory under its control, it will still need support from regional states to sustain itself. The United States and any other nations supporting the opposition will need, at the very least, overflight rights and basing agreements to keep the opposition armed and fed and possibly to provide air support for opposition activities. Of course, supplying the insurgents also will be far easier if the United States can do so by land rather than by air.

Theoretically, any of Iraq's neighbors could serve as a safe haven for the opposition. But, in practice, there are only two realistic choices: Turkey/Kurdistan or Kuwait. Geography and topography make Saudi Arabia, Jordan, and Syria unappealing candidates. The deserts along their borders with Iraq would make insurgent operations extremely difficult and leave them vulnerable to Iraqi counterinsurgency operations—even if assured of considerable U.S. air support. In addition, there are few Iraqi populated areas near those borders, further reducing the ability of insurgents to establish themselves among the civilians and recruit new opposition fighters. The rugged terrain and large numbers of Iraqi towns north of Baghdad make Turkey/Kurdistan an ideal base for the opposition, but Kuwait's proximity to al-Basrah and the marshes around it (to the extent they have not been entirely drained) makes it a plausible if less than ideal second choice. Of course, Iran might be the best choice of all. The Iran–Iraq border is extremely long; in most places the terrain consists of rugged hills, marsh, or mountains; and there are numerous population centers all along it. It should be assumed, however, that U.S.–Iranian relations will not improve quickly enough to make this a viable option within the next few years.

THE NORTHERN SAFE HAVEN. For its part, Turkey generally views Saddam Husayn as a threat to regional security. It would like to see him removed from power, provided that goal can be accomplished without fracturing Iraq or spawning an autonomous Kurdish entity in the North. For the time being, Ankara clearly prefers "the devil it knows," in the person of Saddam Husayn, to the potential for anarchy or a Kurdish state that could result from opposition efforts to overthrow him.

Turkish decision makers tend to believe "their" type of Iraq would be most achievable with the emergence of a new military strongman, one without designs on his neighbors. Nevertheless, if Turkish leaders were convinced that some other form of opposition were both viable and amenable to their vision of Iraq, they might be brought around to support it.

Fearing that failure will strengthen Saddam's motives for revenge, however, Turkish policymakers will be reluctant to adopt this approach in any case. An open embrace of the Iraqi opposition would be a major policy change for Ankara. To convince Turkey would no doubt require costly sweeteners from the United States, among them the following:

- Encouraging opposition leaders to play down discussion of greater Kurdish autonomy, to calm Turkish fears. Indeed, the INC may publicly have to retract its commitment to Kurdish self-determination, or at least make statements that muddy the waters to whatever extent possible.

- Funneling aid to the opposition through Turkey and including Turkish representation in all deliberative and implementing bodies pertaining to this support. This should help convince Ankara that it will be able to prevent the opposition from turning into something threatening to Turkish interests.

- Easing the impact of the UN trade sanctions on Iraq as they apply to Turkey, as has been done for Jordan.

- Working with Congress to see that Turkey is well treated on other issues. This would likely include seeing that Turkey is looked on favorably for arms sales, possibly modifying the traditional balance of U.S. arms sales between Greece and Turkey, lobbying the European Union harder on Ankara's behalf, and so forth.

If the insurgency is to be based in the North, the United States should also work hard to convince the main Kurdish militias to resume full cooperation with the Iraqi opposition. This would greatly improve the northern safe haven's attractiveness; however, such convincing will not be easy. The primary Kurdish militias are often at each other's throats, and they constantly shift their allegiances among Iran, Turkey, Syria, the United States, and the central government in Baghdad. At present, both the Patriotic Union of Kurdistan (PUK) and the Kurdish Democratic Party (KDP) are competing for the attention of the central government, and if this persists, then the opposition would have to be based out of Turkey itself.

Convincing the Kurds to throw their lot in with the opposition again will be difficult. First, the Kurds would have to be convinced that U.S. backing for the effort is strong and enduring. Both the KDP and the PUK leadership feel badly burned by their experiences with Washington from 1991 to 1996. Second, for the opposition to succeed, it must be able to attract Sunni Arab support, which in turn would mean deemphasizing the traditional Kurdish dominance of the INC in favor of a greater Sunni role. Thus, Washington will be asking the Kurds to return to an opposition in which they will have less say than in the past. To bring the KDP and/or the PUK on board with the opposition, the United States and the opposition leadership may have to promise the Kurds autonomy in a future Iraqi state—even while convincing the Kurds to go along with a public retraction of the prior INC commitment to that very goal. Washington also will almost certainly have to offer the Kurds very significant "aid"—in the form of food, humanitarian supplies, consumer goods, and weapons—to secure their cooperation.

THE SOUTHERN SAFE HAVEN. Kuwait could substitute for, or complement, a Turkish/Kurdish sanctuary, although it is less desirable than the northern option. The Kuwaitis remain staunchly opposed to Saddam's regime. If the United States presses them diplomatically and convinces the al-Sabah that (this time) Washington is serious about removing Saddam, the ruling family may support the opposition. Kuwait, however, will question the uncertainties inherent in the "undermine" approach. In particular, having been frustrated by Washington's peripatetic behavior toward the opposition over the past seven years, Kuwait will fear that the United States is once again attempting to oust Saddam "on the cheap" and is not willing to do what is required to remove him. Kuwaiti leaders may decide that it is not worth angering Saddam with a policy that might do little to weaken him; thus they may prefer other U.S.

policy options to "undermine."

For these reasons, a southern safe haven may require the United States to put heavy pressure on Kuwait. Washington will have to convince Kuwait that the strategy has a good chance of success. The administration may also need to convince Kuwait that Americans will not be willing to endure a containment strategy forever nor will they tolerate the costs of an outright invasion; thus, Kuwait's only chance of having the Americans remove Saddam will be to support a U.S. policy aimed at undermining his regime.

In addition, the southern safe haven is less desirable from a military stand point. The border between Iraq and Kuwait is sparsely populated desert. Not until the Euphrates River is there terrain conducive to insurgent or light infantry operations. Iraqi heavy formations would have every advantage in this area, and therefore a southern safe haven approach would place much heavier demands on U.S. airpower much earlier in the insurgent campaign than would be the case if the opposition were based out of the North. The underpopulation of southern Iraq would also make recruiting fighters for the opposition extremely difficult. Only the city of al-Basrah itself could furnish a suitable recruitment base for the opposition, and taking al-Basrah will almost certainly be well beyond opposition capabilities; regime forces are likely to fight very hard to hold their second city, and U.S. air power will largely be impotent in the urban terrain. Consequently, a southern safe haven approach will be more difficult and will take considerably longer to begin to have an impact on the regime than would a northern approach.

Seducing Saddam's Henchmen

This policy option's success would depend as much on the response of Saddam's current supporters as it would on the ability of the Iraqi opposition. To this end, the United States could take several steps to cajole leading Iraqis to turn against Saddam.

To woo Saddam's supporters, Washington could do the following:

- Provide material inducements to those who defect from the regime and/or the armed forces and join the opposition. In particular, opposition fighters should be well-paid, well-armed, and well-provisioned and they should have access to services and supplies that are denied to the regime by the embargo.

- Promise rewards to those who overthrow Saddam. To encourage hesitant coup plotters, the administration could emphasize publicly that the United States would work with *any* friendly successor government. Moreover, Washington should outline a plan for the gradual lifting of sanctions once Saddam has been overthrown.

- Provide covert support to Iraqi coup plotters. The United States could continue efforts to infiltrate Iraq. If the Central Intelligence Agency (CIA) can make contact with senior military or regime officials, it should offer them financial rewards and any logistical help required to help a coup succeed. Such infiltration will be extremely difficult.

- Warn that the United States will encourage any new Iraqi government to deal harshly with all members of the former regime after Saddam's fall, but that it will recommend granting amnesty to those who aid the opposition beforehand.

The composition of the opposition will also play an important role in shaping efforts to convince Iraqis to defect. Although in general, the United States and the Iraqi opposition would be wise to avoid carping on sectarian differences, it is imperative that the opposition be able to influence the behavior of Saddam's power base, whose members are primarily Sunni Arabs from the center and west of the country. This could require a more blatant effort directed specifically at this key constituency. For instance, if the opposition could attract Sunni Arabs to its ranks, it and the United States could then stress the rewards of turning against Saddam and that joining the coalition is their best chance to preserve Sunni prerogatives. On the other hand, if Sunni support were limited, Washington would then have to make a virtue out of necessity and warn that the Sunnis may lose control over Iraq in the event of an opposition victory. In these circumstances, the United States should stress that it will have no incentive to try to protect the Sunni position in Iraq (or even to dissuade a Shi'i- or Kurdish-dominated regime from exacting retribution from Sunni elites). With any luck, such threats could convince Sunni elites to try to preempt an opposition victory by moving against Saddam themselves.

American Military Support

The military objective of this approach is to create an Iraqi opposition force capable of conducting insurgent operations against the central regime—possibly to seize swathes of Iraqi territory sufficient to humiliate the regime. The goal of military operations is both political and psychological, to demonstrate that the regime does not have full control over Iraqi territory and that it is possible to stand up to Saddam. To accomplish this objective will require considerable time and effort. In particular, it will require substantial assistance from the United States in the form of weapons, military supplies, training, and funding.

Nevertheless, one should not overstate the amount of U.S. aid needed to conduct a strategy of undermining Saddam's regime. First, this policy gives the United States the latitude to provide as much or as little support to the opposition as it wants. Second, the military strategy could be essentially defensive: The opposition might be expected simply to conduct guerrilla operations. Finally, because the opposition's guerrilla activities could be used primarily for psychological rather than physical impact, the opposition need only be effective enough to affect Iraqi morale.

A major U.S. military effort, however, *would* be required when and if the opposition proved effective enough to warrant seizing chunks of Iraqi territory, pronouncing them exclusion zones, and then defending them against the regime. Obviously, under a best-case scenario, the opposition fighters would prove so effective that they could shoulder this burden on their own and the United States would have to provide them with logistical support and diplomatic cover only. Yet, given the current state of the opposition and its track record so far, this seems unlikely. More likely, the United States may desire to move the operation along faster than would be required to get the opposition to the necessary level of proficiency to be able to fend for itself. Even with a wealth of anti-tank weapons and good defensive terrain, the opposition will probably be too lightly armed to contend with large Iraqi armored formations by itself. In this case, the United States would have to commit American military forces—mostly in the form of air power—to do much of the work of protecting opposition lines and smashing regime counterattacks.

To accomplish this task, the United States will have to keep several hundred military aircraft in the theater for as long as it takes from the time the opposition first moves into Iraq until Saddam is overthrown. The most demanding task for U.S. air power will be to defeat Iraqi counterattacks, which could consist of several divisions per attack. Warning time for these counterattacks could be slim (at Khafji in 1991, the Iraqis launched an offensive involving three heavy divisions with only a few days of planning and preparation, and the U.S. military did not learn of it until the Iraqi attacks made contact with coalition screening forces). Therefore, the forces required to defeat such thrusts will have to be in-theater and available at all times. Even with the latest weaponry, it could require anywhere from 200 to 500 sorties over the course of one to three days to halt such an Iraqi counterattack (Khafji required 1,000 strike sorties in three days). To generate this volume of sorties will require at least 200 to 300 strike aircraft, plus an equal number of air superiority, logistics, and C⁴I (command, control, communications, computers, and intelligence) planes. The United States would have to expect to keep these forces in place, patrolling Iraq, suppressing Iraqi air defenses, interdicting Iraqi military movements, and smashing periodic Iraqi counterattacks for many months if not several years. In addition, the United States will have to deploy special forces personnel with the opposition forces to provide training, serve as advisers, and probably act as forward air controllers as well.

These forces will also need basing in the region. The farther from the operating zones they are based, the more aircraft will be required to compensate for time spent flying to and from the combat zone. If a southern safe haven option is pursued, the United States could employ aircraft carriers in the Gulf to provide part of the air contingent. Yet, the difficulty of keeping carriers on station in the Gulf and the global scale of American naval commitments will mean that the United States will rarely be able to maintain more than two carriers on station, which could provide only a small part of the needed air forces.

Managing Diplomatic Reaction

A strategy aimed at undermining Saddam's regime will unfold mostly within Iraq but will have an impact on a wide variety of other states. The United States cannot expect the rest of the world simply to ignore an American effort to topple Saddam by building a vigorous Iraqi opposition. Washington will also have to create the proper diplomatic environment for this strategy to bear fruit. Obviously, the most important goal of U.S. diplomacy must be to secure the requisite safe haven for the opposition. Yet, there are at least two other key diplomatic criteria: First, Saddam must be kept weak and isolated to give the opposition the chance to build its strength and destabilize his regime; and second, other states, particularly great powers, must be convinced to support the opposition actively or, at the least, not to interfere with it.

KEEPING SADDAM CONTAINED. Although "undermine" is an offensive strategy, it requires a defensive component as well. It may be several years before the Iraqi opposition is ready to take the field against Saddam. During that time, it is imperative that at least some form of containment—particularly the sanctions and inspections regimes—be maintained. The United States could not simply "junk" containment in favor of an approach aimed at undermining the regime, because such an approach cannot promise quick success—if it succeeds at all. During the interim, while Saddam is still in power, Washington will still need to limit Iraq's freedom of action to prevent it from destabilizing the Gulf. The United States cannot simply let Saddam loose in the Gulf while it works to oust him: Washington will have to continue to enforce the defensive strategy of containment at the same time as it attempts the offensive strategy of undermining the regime.

Containment is also critical to keep Saddam weak and to ensure that the opposition has a realistic chance of getting rid of the regime. The lifting of sanctions and/or the end of the inspections would be an enormous victory for Saddam domestically. It would allow him to claim (quite rightly) that his strategy for handling the UN and the United States was correct and that confrontation paid off. An Iraqi populace that has just had its economic welfare restored and seen Saddam's resistance to the UN crowned with success is not going to be a people eager to join the opposition. In addition, ending the sanctions would provide Saddam with the resources to rebuild his armed forces and his WMD arsenal. The stronger the Iraqi armed forces are, the harder it will be for the opposition to conduct insurgent operations. The greater the threat of Iraqi conventional and nonconventional forces, the less likely some of Iraq's neighbors will be to anger Baghdad by supporting the opposition. In these circumstances, it would be far more difficult for the opposition to recruit new members and to bring any pressure against the regime. For these reasons, the likelihood of successfully undermining Saddam's regime is directly linked to the strength of containment.

Ensuring that containment remains intact for the period of years needed for this option to work (and it is hardly guaranteed that it *will* work) will mean treading lightly to keep the international coalition together. The United States may have to refrain from taking provocative actions against Iraq, even if Washington may believe doing so would best block Iraqi machinations. For example, so as not to fracture the coalition, the United States will be constrained in its ability to use military force in response to Iraqi challenges to the sanctions or inspections.

These limitations will extend even to U.S. support for the opposition itself. There are a wide variety of actions that, in theory, could be useful to the opposition, but that in practice could undermine containment. For instance, it may not be prudent to try to fund the opposition by transferring frozen Iraqi assets to them. Doing so would be a violation of international law that could lead Iraq's advocates in the UN to break with the United States on sanctions and inspections enforcement. Indeed, even such actions as pushing to have Saddam indicted as a war criminal could redound against this policy: If a vigorous American campaign were to alienate France, Russia, and China, it could erode containment without having much impact on the opposition's prospects against Saddam. Likewise, if Iraqi elites feared that they too would be indicted for war crimes, they would be more likely to rally around Saddam than to defect to the opposition.

Thus there is a direct relationship between containment

and support for the opposition: A strategy designed to undermine the regime requires containment of one sort or another to keep Saddam pinned while the opposition rebuilds, to keep him vulnerable to the opposition, and as a "fail-safe" in the event the opposition is unable to bring about his downfall. Yet, the sanctions and inspections regime is an obvious and vulnerable target: Iraq and its advocates will undoubtedly attack them in response to efforts to support the opposition against Baghdad. The harder the United States pushes the opposition, the harder Iraq will go after the sanctions, and potentially, the more weight its arguments will carry with other Security Council members. Consequently, the more aggressive U.S. support is to the opposition, the more difficult it will be to maintain a strong containment regime. This suggests that, if the United States were to pursue a more aggressive version of undermining the regime, it should simultaneously move toward narrow containment, which would minimize that policy's reliance on the Security Council and thus reduce its vulnerability. On the other hand, if the United States intended to provide only modest support to the opposition, it probably could do so in the context of broad containment, as there would be less pressure in the Security Council.

KEEPING AMERICA'S ALLIES FROM INTERFERING. Any offensive U.S. policy toward Iraq will require considerable cooperation from regional states. "Undermine" is no exception. In light of Washington's relative neglect of the Iraqi opposition in the past, however, this could prove a formidable task. The United States will likely have to devote much diplomatic energy to convince regional states that it is serious about the opposition this time. Even this may not be enough, and it may require the United States to make compromises on other issues to secure the needed regional support.

The active participation of regional states other than Turkey and Kuwait would be useful but not critical to an approach aimed at undermining Saddam Husayn. They would be asked only to provide aid—diplomatic, financial, and perhaps military. Other Arab states could provide a useful veneer of legitimacy to the opposition by publicly supporting its efforts to topple Saddam. Likewise, the U.S. treasury would clearly benefit from any financial assistance the Gulf states would be willing to furnish. Finally, some Arab states might be prevailed upon to give small arms, anti-tank weapons, and man-portable anti-aircraft weapons to the insurgents. Indeed, it would be useful for political reasons to have Egyptian and Jordanian special forces personnel participate in training the opposition fighters.

Convincing regional states to support the U.S. effort on behalf of the opposition will be difficult, however. The suffering of the Iraqi people has gained Baghdad support throughout the Middle East, and other Arab governments will be loath to back a bloody strategy that will take years to bear fruit—if it does so at all—while their publics agitate for Iraq's rehabilitation. Moreover, most Middle Eastern governments have become convinced that the United States will not do what is required to ensure that Saddam is overthrown, and they may see the strategy as an effort to avoid hard choices.

The United States may find itself unable to drum up much support for such a strategy. American allies in the region may be uncomfortable with any additional U.S. military presence directly associated with the "undermine" option and may grow increasingly critical of the policy over time. Because this policy will be associated with the United States, regional populaces may oppose it as a form of neocolonialism. Also, the time required for the strategy to work—and the lack of a definitive end game—will make opposition to the strategy an enduring source of friction in the region. Therefore, it will be critical for Washington to make sure that regional allies do not publicly oppose the U.S. policy. Just as their support would give the opposition an important source of legitimacy, which would increase their appeal within Iraq, so Arab animosity to the opposition would discredit it among Iraqis.

A policy designed to undermine Saddam's regime could have even greater difficulty garnering support outside the Gulf region, and the United States will probably have to expend considerable political capital to prevent the policy from failing. Russia, China, and France will almost certainly accuse the United States of going beyond the UN mandate, and they could respond by pressing for the lifting of sanctions. Realistically, Washington's diplomatic objectives should be not to convince these powers to join the U.S. effort but to persuade them not to oppose it actively or use it to justify lifting the sanctions.

To prevent such developments, the United States will have to lobby its allies and other powers, and it may have to make sacrifices elsewhere around the globe. The United States should emphasize that undermining the regime may eventually rid the world of Saddam, thus ending the isolation of Iraq. The alternative, it should be stressed, will be continued conflict and containment. Washington should also be prepared to make tradeoffs in other foreign policy areas. Both U.S. allies and other great powers may demand *quid pro quo*s in exchange for their support or neutrality. Thus, Washington may have to make concessions on issues such as the pace of North Atlantic Treaty Organization (NATO) expansion, the admittance of China into the World Trade Organization, and restrictions on U.S. agriculture exports to Europe.

Can it Work?

To achieve its maximum goals, "undermine" relies on Iraqi government elites to remove Saddam from power. There is no mechanism for removing Saddam. The policy is designed to create instability in Iraq by supporting the opposition, but it does not envision that the opposition will necessarily be strong enough to march on Baghdad and take power itself. Instead, the policy assumes that creating such instability should be adequate to prompt an assassination or coup d'état that would remove Saddam. Thus a critical question is whether it is reasonable to expect that, if the opposition is able to create widespread instability in Baghdad, this would prompt Saddam's supporters to move against him.

Convincing Iraqi elites to stage an assassination or a coup will not be easy. Saddam is protected by a terrifying security apparatus that watches over all of Iraq and focuses particular attention on the military and other elements of Saddam's power base. The Iraqi military is thoroughly politicized: Saddam has not hesitated to relieve or even execute any general who shows an independent bent. Any individual who seeks to overthrow or assassinate Saddam is aware of the hundreds of thousands of previous coup plotters, would-be assassins, insurgents, and innocents whom Saddam has murdered.

The historical evidence bears out the daunting challenges this policy will face. For several reasons, building an opposition army in a security zone in or near Iraq probably would face significant hurdles trying to bring about Saddam's downfall. First, Saddam probably will not destroy himself by attacking the security zones and so expose his forces to pounding by U.S. air forces. In the last seven years, Saddam has shown surprising patience, often waiting out the United States and its local allies and generally refraining from operations that would provide the United States with an opening to move against him with massive force. Second, such an approach has been tried and has failed in the past. From 1992 to 1996, the INC held an enclave in northern Iraq. The Iraqi military was kept out of this zone, and all Iraqis—both in the opposition and in Baghdad—believed the United States would use air power to defend it. Nonetheless, Iraqi units did not defect *en masse* and most regime supporters saw this enclave as a U.S. attempt to divide Iraq and end Sunni Arab domination of the country.

Despite the pervasive fear of Saddam's security services, however, the regime *has* faced regular challenges to its rule. Cabals of army and Republican Guard officers, high-ranking regime officials, and elements of Saddam's core Sunni tribes have all made bids to topple him at various times. In fact, since the Gulf War there has not been a single year when Saddam did not face at least one serious coup attempt. In particular, a policy of supporting the opposition would be most likely to spark a coup attempt against Saddam if it could successfully convince Saddam's supporters of the following:

- Their own security would be in jeopardy if they did not oust him. If a U.S.-backed opposition appears to be gaining ground, Saddam's cronies may fear for their lives and those of their families. Thus, they may seek to preempt an opposition take-over by removing Saddam from power themselves.
- The status of their communities was in jeopardy. Saddam's Iraq is dominated by Sunni Arabs, and the regime itself is run by a core of Saddam's relatives, members of the al-Bu Nasir tribe, and individuals from a small number of other, mostly Sunni Arab, tribes. All of these groups would likely lose their privileges if the opposition were to triumph.
- Saddam can no longer maintain internal stability. If the opposition becomes an effective thorn in Iraq's side, this will diminish Saddam's stature and lead to frustration and disgruntlement among Iraqi elites. Ensuring Iraq's internal stability is a priority for most Iraqi elites, and Saddam's failure to do so could lead his current supporters to turn against him.
- Betrayal has its rewards. If the United States and the opposition are willing to reward Saddam's henchmen rather than punish them, they will be more willing to take action against him.

END STATE

The end game of "undermine" is to see Saddam Husayn out of

power. This is essentially the limit of the policy's desired end state: It is a policy intended to leave "anyone but Saddam" running Iraq. If the opposition were somehow to take power in the wake of Saddam's fall, this would certainly be preferable and the United States should encourage it. Nevertheless, the policy recognizes that this may not be a likely outcome and that attempting to improve significantly the opposition's chances of taking power would require exponentially greater commitments of American resources and, possibly, military power. (For a discussion of this issue, see the annex on "Overthrowing Saddam.")

ADVANTAGES

A policy designed to undermine Saddam Husayn's regime would have the following advantages:

- *End Saddam's rule.* By removing Saddam from power, Iraq's foreign policy is likely to become less aggressive and less hostile to the West. Moreover, Saddam himself is a vengeful person: His removal reduces the chances that Iraq will support terrorism or strike at Saddam's personal opponents. Any successor regime probably will also be less brutal at home.

- *Support an Iraqi opposition, thus placing the onus for Iraq's future on the Iraqi people.* The United States will bear some responsibility for the new regime, but less than if it imposed the government directly (see "Invade").

- *Raise pressure on Saddam.* Even if the policy does not succeed in ousting Saddam, it will weaken his regime, forcing him to devote his already-limited resources to suppressing unrest. Moreover, the United States can increase or decrease support for the opposition as a way of coercing Saddam, raising the heat if the dictator tries any aggressive acts.

- *Limit the commitment of U.S. resources.* The degree of support the United States provides the opposition could be kept limited while still achieving the aim of pressuring Saddam. Or, if appropriate, because the opposition is doing well or because Saddam is posing more of a threat, the support could be increased to the level needed to achieve an opposition victory.

LIABILITIES AND RISKS

On the other hand, among the policy's disadvantages are the fact that it would do the following:

- *Continue the need for containment.* "Undermine" is not a substitute for containment, only a supplement to it. In the years required to make this policy work, the United States will have to sustain containment to keep the regime weak and vulnerable to the opposition.

- *Complicate broad containment.* "Undermine" could lead U.S. allies and the United Nations to become even more dissatisfied with U.S. policy. There is a high risk that the UN Special Commission on Iraq (UNSCOM) and other UN-based efforts to enforce Iraqi compliance with the various UN resolutions would collapse. U.S. abandonment of efforts to work within the UN framework—after years of justifying U.S. policy in the name of UN resolutions—might lead other powers to scorn the United Nations, making it even less effective. On the other hand, the policy might still work in conjunction with a more narrow variant of containment.

- *Involve a high likelihood of failure.* Given the current weakness of Iraqi opposition groups, their disappointing track record, and the fact that the United States does not have access to Iraq's inner circles, it could prove very difficult to make this policy work. To the extent that "undermine" relies on creating the circumstances in which someone will overthrow Saddam, it faces the problem that fomenting a coup or provoking an assassination attempt is inherently difficult to accomplish.

- *Not provide a quick-fix.* Undermining the current regime does not offer a quick solution to the problem of Iraq. It could take years to rebuild the Iraqi opposition or create an INC military force capable of even the most basic guerrilla operations against the regime. Even if the opposition progresses to the point at which it could seize and hold portions of Iraq, it could be years before this would lead to a successful coup, much less an opposition victory.
- *Allow for the possibility of "backlash."* Overt U.S. support for an Iraqi opposition based largely on Kurds or Shi'i Arabs could discredit the movement among the very people it is intended to win over—the regime's Sunni core. Iraqi elites could rally around Saddam as the opposition grows in strength, seeing him as the last bulwark against their own subjugation.
- *Have little likelihood of promoting good government.* Even if Saddam did fall because of such a strategy, the opposition probably would not take power as a result. Because this policy approach relies on others to bring about Saddam's fall—and the opposition would likely be distant from Baghdad—the power struggle that ensued would not necessarily favor the opposition. Thus, others in Iraq, such as elements of the Republican Guard, the intelligence services, or the Ba'th party, would be much better positioned to take power. Any of these sorts would be likely to continue a high level of repression in Iraq and probably would share Saddam's dreams of leading the Arab world (though they may be more cautious in pursuing this dream) and acquiring weapons of mass destruction.
- *Foster instability in Iraq.* By undermining the central government of Iraq without installing any replacement, the United States may inadvertently be fostering a long-term period of instability in Iraq. In general, insurgencies are better for destabilizing a country than they are for install-

ing the government preferred by the intervening power. Supporting insurgents in Iraq also might lead to the collapse of central government authority altogether, turning the country into another Lebanon or Afghanistan.

- *Lead to genocide.* To keep the opposition from gaining ground, Saddam will kill or forcibly relocate any potential sympathizers. In the past, he has repeatedly crushed lightly armed opposition forces. Moreover, he has not hesitated to slaughter any Iraqis who support the insurgency: To paraphrase Mao, Saddam will try to dry up the sea in which the guerrillas swim. He has literally done this in Iraq's southern marshes.

- *Leave the United States with few remaining options if the policy fails.* Washington may be faced with the unwanted choice of either relying on deterrence alone to stop Saddam or else invading Iraq with U.S. forces. This would be especially true if aggressive U.S. support for the opposition undermines the containment regime.

- *Place heavy demands on the U.S. military.* "Undermine" could require a far more extensive and sustained U.S. military presence in the Gulf than exists at present. U.S. operational tempo, already high, would increase even further.

- *Incite opposition from Iran.* The regime in Tehran may strongly oppose a policy designed to undermine the Iraqi regime. Iran prefers the current state of Iraq: weak but united. If Saddam were assassinated, Tehran may fear that Iraq's isolation would end and that his successors would rebuild Iraq and again threaten the Islamic Republic. Given the poor state of U.S.–Iranian relations today, Tehran's opposition matters little, but this policy could interfere with any U.S.–Iran rapprochement.

CONCLUSIONS

A decision to back the opposition in a bid to topple the regime offers hope for a Persian Gulf without the threat of Saddam Husayn. Moreover, it promises to do so at an affordable price, and without U.S. casualties. At the same time, it would be difficult to implement and could lead to serious problems. "Undermine" has only a modest potential actually to end the "problem of Saddam." Moreover, such a policy is not for the faint of heart. It would generate a storm of criticism from U.S. allies and raise doubts at home. It is a risky strategy that will not pay off for years, if ever.

For these reasons, a policy of undermining Saddam Husayn might best serve not as a substitute for, but as an adjunct to, current U.S. policy. From this perspective, support to the opposition would increase the pressure on Saddam at a cost to the United States that could be kept low. Attempts to undermine the regime could help coerce Saddam into compliance with the UN resolutions. The policy would function as a more active and aggressive form of containment. As long as the United States recognized it as such, was willing to pay the price in terms of resources allocated and casualties (mainly to the opposition), and could convince its allies to support such an approach, this could prove an effective source of leverage to strengthen the containment regime.

ANNEX: OVERTHROWING SADDAM

It is conceivable that the Iraqi opposition could be used not merely to pressure Saddam or create the circum stances for a coup, but actually to do the job themselves. The basic premise of such an effort would be to employ sufficient U.S. military power to help the Iraqi opposition actually overthrow Saddam Husayn in a conventional military campaign. Although this policy shares many characteristics with the "undermine" approach, "overthrow" also has many important differences stemming from the distinct goals of the two policies. Undermine simply attempts both to strengthen the opposition enough to create instability in Iraq and to create the conditions under which Saddam might be toppled—probably by someone other than the opposition. This is a relatively low risk and low cost—but also low probability—approach. By contrast, overthrow is designed to improve the probability of successfully ousting Saddam, but at greater risk and cost.

Overthrow also offers several advantages compared to other options. By providing the opposition with the military support to overthrow Saddam, the United States could shape a future Iraqi regime. Thus, the United States would have a greater degree of assurance that a successor government would be amenable to U.S. regional interests and respectful of human rights. Similarly, in contrast to an invasion strategy, overthrowing the regime through the use of domestic opposition would not place the onus of creating a new government in Iraq *completely* on the United States and would involve few U.S. casualties, as the brunt of the fighting would be done by Iraqis, not Americans.

Nevertheless, an overthrow policy is ambitious. In addition to arming and training an opposition army, the United States would have to help it conquer Iraq. This would require massive amounts of U.S. airpower, as the opposition forces will be limited in both numbers and skill. To sustain operations, the United States would require bases in the region for training the opposition and for supporting U.S. airpower. In addition to the massive amounts of resources required, such a policy is difficult to implement and will face opposition from U.S. allies.

SIMILARITIES TO UNDERMINE . . .

A policy designed to overthrow the Iraqi regime would share many similarities with one aimed at undermining it, because both options employ support to the Iraqi opposition as their principal mechanism. Like undermine, overthrow would entail the following:

- Revamping the Iraqi opposition to turn it into a viable political and military force able to contest Saddam Husayn's power.
- Securing enough assistance from U.S. allies in the region to provide the opposition with a safe haven and U.S. forces with bases from which to operate against the Iraqi regime. Moreover, as with undermine, Turkey and Kuwait would be the best candidates for both safe havens and military bases.
- Aiding the opposition diplomatically and financially, and helping it to gain the support of the Iraqi people.
- Managing world and domestic public opinion to ensure that U.S. policy is sustainable and does not lead to unanticipated diplomatic costs.

. . . AND DIFFERENCES

Yet, designing a policy to overthrow the regime is somewhat different from designing one to undermine it, because the two policies' goals are very different. Consequently, despite the broad areas of overlap, there are also important distinctions between the two approaches.

A Pluralist Opposition

Unlike undermine, if the United States were to pursue the overthrow option, realistically, it could not accept "anyone but Saddam" in power in Baghdad. Because the United States will be making a massive commitment of resources and risking American casualties, Washington almost certainly will have to ensure that any successor regime will have at least a vague air of pluralism about it. The United States may not require an Iraqi Thomas Jefferson to take over from Saddam, but the Iraqi opposition will have to be relatively broad-based and allow at least some popular input into decision making. This will necessitate a more drastic revamping of the Iraqi opposition than envisaged by the undermine approach.

Of course, a more balanced opposition will also have advantages for the United States. It will be more attractive in the region, easing both Turkish and Iranian fears of a Kurdish-dominated resistance movement and Saudi and Kuwaiti concerns over a Shi'a-dominated opposition. Likewise, a broad-based opposition would also be more likely to garner support in Iraq itself and would lessen the risk that any one communal group (particularly the Sunnis) would turn to Saddam to protect them from their ethnic rivals. Finally, a broad base would minimize the inevitable charges that the movement is a U.S. puppet rather than a legitimate expression of the Iraqi people.

A Larger American Military Effort

Probably the greatest difference between an approach designed to undermine and one designed to overthrow the regime would be the extent of U.S. military operations required to make overthrow work. The success of an overthrow policy would rest ultimately on a two-stage military campaign. In the first stage the United States would arm and train the Iraqi opposition. An opposition capable of undermining Saddam, however, would require at least two divisions' worth of reasonably well-trained and well-armed opposition fighters—possibly more. Based on the current state of the Iraqi opposition and America's historical experience in aiding popular insurgencies, it would require at least six months to train each cohort of Iraqi opposition fighters and at least two to four years to recruit and train all of the cohorts necessary to fill two divisions' worth of opposition fighters. During this time, the emphasis would be on recruiting and training the opposition forces in security zones in Kuwait, Turkey, or Iraq itself; U.S. military operations would therefore focus on keeping Iraqi forces at bay while the opposition trained.

In the second stage, U.S. air power would be used to "break" Iraqi government forces, and the opposition would then occupy the territory once the government units collapsed. Ideally, opposition successes would lead to mass defections from the Iraqi army (as happened after Desert Storm), causing the opposition's ranks to swell. The military goal of the opposition forces would be to move steadily toward Baghdad, attracting Iraqi army defectors along the way. Rather than use guerrilla tactics (as in the undermine approach), the opposition would engage in a conventional conflict against regime forces. Depending on the rate of defections, the skill of the opposition forces, and the extent of U.S. air power employed, such a campaign would take several months at least.

U.S. air power is necessary if the opposition is to succeed. Indeed, air power will do the lion's share of the work. The amount of air power employed will depend on the strength of the opposition: A stronger opposition will require less air support, whereas a weak opposition may rely heavily on U.S. air strikes to smash Iraqi combat formations and defend the opposition forces from counterattack. U.S. strikes on Iraqi forces will have an important psychological effect as well. They will convince Iraqi military leaders that Saddam's continued presence poses a threat to their own survival. The rank and file also may defect more readily to escape U.S. attacks. The demands on U.S. air power would be tremendous. The United States would be attempting a feat that has proven elusive throughout military history: forcing a rival regime to capitulate almost entirely through air power. In particular, the air campaign will have to take the burden of fighting off the opposition ground forces by flying large numbers of close air support (CAS) and battlefield air interdiction (BAI) missions to paralyze regime operations and to "crack" regime combat formations. Thus, the air operations for supporting an opposition in Iraq would in some ways be more demanding than those of Desert Storm, for the following reasons:

- U.S. air forces would be operating in support of relatively untrained, lightly armed Iraqi opposition combatants, not U.S. ground forces. In many cases, cracking Iraqi army units sufficiently for opposition ground forces to triumph would probably require greater attrition and damage than was inflicted in Desert Storm. It should be noted that the Republican Guard divisions never "broke" under air attack during Desert Storm, even though several of them were subjected to more than 1,000 sorties each.

- CAS is particularly difficult when ground and air units do not share common procedures—a problem likely to plague U.S. coordination with opposition troops. U.S. advisers probably will have to serve as forward air controllers.

- The logistical requirements would be demanding, as the United States would be operating with less local support and farther into hostile territory than it did in Operation Desert Storm.

As a result, the military forces the United States will require for these operations would be considerable. Several hundred sorties per day would be needed for months to provide CAS and BAI for the opposition ground forces. In addition, on numerous occasions, the United States will have to increase its air operations greatly, either to pave the way for opposition ground offensives or to defeat regime counterattacks. On such occasions, the United States will likely have to "surge" at least 400 to 500 strike sorties per day for several days at a time—often with very little warning time. In addition, the United States will have to provide air superiority fighters to ensure that the Iraqi Air Force is kept on the ground, jammers and air-defense suppression aircraft to handle Iraq's ground-based air defenses, airborne warning and control systems (AWACS) and joint surveillance target attack radar systems (JSTARS) to control the operation, tankers to keep the planes flying, other reconnaissance aircraft to ensure information dominance, and transports to move people and supplies around the theater. Altogether these various missions will require a U.S. air effort of anywhere from 500 to 1,200 aircraft. In addition, the United States will have to deploy several battalions of special operations forces to train the Iraqi opposition and serve as advisers, forward air controllers, and liaisons for opposition field forces.

The total time required for these operations will vary according to the opposition's strength, the rate of defections, and the amount of air power the United States can deploy. It will take roughly twelve to twenty-four months to train Iraqi forces once sufficient numbers have been recruited. During this training period, the U.S. military will have to defend the haven where the opposition is based. Once the insurgents are ready to take the offensive, the United States should plan for a campaign lasting months, not weeks. Part of the goal of the operations is to foster defections among Saddam's forces—a goal that will take time. The opposition forces, even after training, are not likely to be able to conduct rapid and sustained operations. Moreover, cracking the Iraqi armed forces through air power is difficult and time-consuming, if it can be done at all. Military operations will involve scores to hundreds of U.S. casualties.

The United States also will have to prepare for the possibility—or perhaps even the probability—that Saddam will escalate should the opposition appear to be succeeding. Saddam's escalation could involve attacks on Israel, Kuwait, Saudi Arabia, or other U.S. allies. If Saddam's back is up against the wall, he might even resort to terrorism or chemical or biological strikes. To deter such escalation, or to respond to it should deterrence fail, the United States will require even more substantial military forces. Given existing technological and intelligence limits, it is possible that such assets will not prevent Saddam from escalating.

An Overt Strategy

An undermine strategy could, at least in theory, remain covert. At the very least, U.S. involvement could be kept to a level that would preserve American "plausible deniability." On the other hand, an overthrow strategy would have to be overt. For the opposition to achieve the goals of the overthrow option, the United States will have to commit large numbers of air strikes to attrit and demoralize Iraqi government forces and pave the way for opposition ground units. Given the massive nature of the U.S. effort, overthrow could not work as a covert strategy. Overthrow envisions a war against Iraq—one fought primarily by Iraqi ground troops, but with no less obviously American involvement than under the Nixon administration strategy of "Vietnamization."

The fact that overthrow envisions large-scale, overt U.S. military operations against Iraq creates numerous hurdles, which an undermine strategy would not have to clear. An overthrow policy would give the Iraqi opposition the comfort of massive U.S. fire power, but it would also make crystal clear that the opposition was a tool of the United States. There could be no disguising the fact that it would ride to power on the coattails of the U.S. Air Force. This might make it less popular among Iraqis, even though it is clear that many Iraqis—probably most—would welcome the end of Saddam, the end of Iraq's diplomatic isolation, and the restoration of good relations with the United States. It could also make enemies out of other regional states—such as Syria or possibly Iran—which may be loath to border a country considered an American "puppet."

A LIKELY END TO CONTAINMENT. If the United States were to adopt a policy of overthrow, it could easily mean an end to the international containment of Iraq. Most of the international community would probably split with the United States for having made a mockery of the notion of international coordination through the UN to determine collective actions against Iraq. Arab publics will probably see this as blatant American aggression, and they could make it difficult for their governments to actively support the Iraqi opposition or U.S. military operations against Saddam. A U.S. war against Iraq could well mean the end of sanctions, and it would be extremely difficult to maintain the UNSCOM inspections, as Iraq would have little incentive to continue to comply with the UN resolutions. If anything, the United Nations might turn into a vehicle for the Iraqi government, providing it with a forum from which to denounce the United States. As the United States would have to keep Saddam pinned down until the opposition was ready, Washington could find itself enforcing containment unilaterally—using the U.S. military to intercept trucks coming across Iraq's borders or ships in the Gulf headed for Iraqi ports.

If pursuing a policy of overthrow resulted in the end of containment, this would greatly complicate U.S. policy toward Iraq, but it would also carry some advantages—advantages that would not accrue to an undermine approach. In particular, Washington could take a series of actions to bolster the opposition— actions from which it now refrains because they could erode the sanctions and inspections regimes. The United States could indict Saddam as a war criminal, seize Iraqi assets and use them to fund the training and equipping of the opposition, declare Iraqi territory captured by the opposition to be "free Iraq," and/or recognize the opposition as the legitimate government of Iraq.

Thus, pursuing an overthrow strategy would free the United States from the need to make its policies conform, even broadly, to the desires of the rest of the UN Security Council.

TOUGHER DIPLOMATIC PROBLEMS. Because the U.S. military effort in support of the opposition would be blatant, overthrow would put a greater burden on U.S. diplomacy. Unlike undermine, in which criticism would be widespread but probably muted, overthrow would likely stir up widespread and vehement international opprobrium. In particular, other states may object to not only the extent of U.S. military intervention but also its likely protracted length and lack of a guaranteed end game; at least with an invasion, they may argue, the killing would be over quickly and the end of Saddam would be a certainty.

The most important U.S. diplomatic goal must be to ensure the passivity of various important powers, particularly Russia and China. These countries need not support U.S. policy, but they should be strongly discouraged from aiding the Iraqi government in any way. Managing key powers and important allies will require a mix of blandishments and pressure. U.S. leaders could make clear to countries such as Russia and China, which depend heavily on U.S. investment and the U.S. market, that strong economic relations are contingent on their noninterference with U.S. policy in the Gulf. Washington might consider concessions on other important foreign policy areas in exchange for noninterference with U.S. policy toward Iraq. The United States could also encourage the opposition leadership to promise future oil contracts to French, Russian, and Chinese entities to give them an incentive to support an opposition victory.

Those American allies that support the overthrow of

Saddam Husayn should be encouraged to play an active role. Japan, Britain, Canada, and probably Kuwait appear likely to give at least grudging support. In this case, Britain and Canada might be asked to provide air support and help train Iraqi insurgents (indeed, the British military has often excelled at training developing-world militaries). Japan might be asked to help pay the cost of the overall effort. Of course, such support would be very useful, but would not be essential for an overthrow policy to succeed.

Finally, securing basing for U.S. warplanes will also be a key challenge for American diplomacy, and it could prove a major constraint on U.S. military operations. The United States will have to convince one or more of Iraq's neighbors to allow it to conduct a sustained air campaign from their airfields, something most have been reluctant to do since the Gulf War. Longer-range support aircraft (such as JSTARS, AWACS, and tankers) could be based farther from Iraq, such as in the Gulf Cooperation Council (GCC) states, but the rest will have to be deployed to Saudi Arabia, Kuwait, Turkey, and/or Jordan. Moreover, without bases in Turkey, sustained operations against northern Iraq probably would not be possible, unless Apache helicopters and perhaps Marine Harriers could be deployed directly to Iraqi Kurdistan or an air base constructed in opposition-held territory. For a southern safe haven approach, even if Kuwait were to provide full access to its bases, it is highly likely that the United States would have to increase capacity at the Kuwaiti air bases and perhaps seize or build new bases in Iraq itself to provide adequate ramp space for the air fleet.

Carriers in the Persian Gulf could be used to supplement land-based air forces (although only in support of a southern safe haven approach), but they would not be adequate to bear the brunt of the air effort alone—even if carrier air wings were reconfigured to include only strike aircraft because U.S. support aircraft were able to fly from nearby ground bases. The

United States would need anywhere from four to ten carriers to generate the needed amount of combat sorties depending on the threat environment. As there are only ten active carrier air wings in the U.S. Navy's order of battle, and it is impractical to have more than two carriers deployed in the Gulf region for sustained periods of time, it would be impossible to execute this strategy effectively without considerable ground air bases near Iraq.

Because basing is such an important requirement of a strategy to overthrow the regime, regional diplomacy would be of even greater importance than it would be for a strategy to undermine it. Undermine envisions U.S. air support only as a possibility and only at the end of a long process in which the opposition forces themselves will have done most of the work. An overthrow strategy, however, places the onus on U.S. air power and does so right from the start. For these reasons, Turkish, Kuwaiti, Jordanian, and Saudi concerns would merit particularly close attention. None of these countries is likely to favor an overthrow approach—if Washington could convince them that a strong anti-Saddam policy is necessary, they all would probably prefer a U.S. invasion to a long, protracted, internal war backed by the United States. Thus, U.S. diplomacy will have to pull out all of the stops to convince one or more of these states to support the effort wholeheartedly. This could require making considerable economic concessions to Amman, making concessions to Ankara on arms sales, and convincing Riyadh and Kuwait that the American public will no longer support containment but that it will not yet support an invasion, thus making overthrow the only possible alternative to pure deterrence.

CONCLUSIONS

If the United States is determined to see Saddam Husayn gone from power without actually committing U.S. ground troops to an invasion of Iraq, then it should seek to overthrow—not undermine—the regime. Overthrow offers a much greater likelihood that Saddam will be removed from power than undermine, and it also gives Washington a greater say in the shape of an Iraqi successor regime. Overthrow relies on opposition forces—rather than U.S. soldiers—to do the brunt of the ground fighting. Supporting a broad-based opposition thus strikes the right balance between America's liberal ideals and concern for the safety of American soldiers. Limited American casualties will also help to maintain U.S. domestic support for a sizable military presence in the Persian Gulf.

On the other hand, overthrow is a far more costly and risky strategy than undermine. Helping the opposition to victory would require an air campaign of Desert Storm proportions and it is not clear that even such an effort would be sufficient to do the job. Iraq could respond by employing weapons of mass destruction, supporting terrorism, or both. Indeed, to stay in power, Saddam will also commit atrocities of genocidal proportions within Iraq. Overthrow risks the disintegration of Iraq, leaving the country looking like another Lebanon or Afghanistan. Nor is it clear that the United States can control the opposition. Allies in the region and throughout the world will oppose an overthrow policy. Regional allies fear instability and worry that strife in Iraq will spread to their own countries. European and Asian allies would also oppose an overthrow policy, seeing it as untenable and perhaps leading to a U.S.-dominated government. Finally, an overthrow approach would complicate "broad" containment, as it could lead U.S. allies and the United Nations to become even more dissatisfied with U.S. policy. UNSCOM and other UN-based efforts to weaken and contain Iraq could collapse.

Chapter 4

DETER
Putting Iraq in Perspective

Andrew T. Parasiliti

Deterrence argues that the United States should deemphasize Iraq as a foreign policy problem and handle any potential Iraqi challenge to U.S. interests and allies with the threat of military force. According to this policy, the United States would establish clear red lines regarding Iraqi behavior: Any threatening troop movements against Kuwait or Saudi Arabia (and perhaps Jordan), any open deployment or use of chemical or biological weapons, or any act of Iraqi-sponsored terrorism against the United States would be met with a U.S. military response. That being said, deterrence suggests that U.S. interests in the Persian Gulf are best served through a regional approach to collective security supported by a credible U.S. military deterrent.

A policy of deterrence assumes that containment is no longer a viable long-term strategy for dealing with Iraq. Since August 1996, when Saddam Husayn's troops entered Iraqi Kurdistan at the invitation of Masoud Barzani's Kurdish Democratic Party (KDP), U.S. containment strategy toward Iraq has suffered a series of body blows that have raised questions about the policy's durability. The latest round of U.S.–Iraq confrontation, culminating in the February 1998 memorandum of understanding (MOU) between Iraq and United Nations secretary general Kofi Annan, revealed a number of challenges to the current containment regime, including a strengthened Saddam Husayn and fraying UN and Arab support for U.S. policy. Many in the Arab world and elsewhere are uneasy with a UN sanctions regime that creates undue hardships for the Iraqi people while Saddam's hold on power appears to be unaffected.

Also troubling is that containment grants the initiative to Saddam Husayn, resulting in a crisis-driven, reactive U.S. foreign policy in a region where long-term strategic vision is vital. Furthermore, the American obsession with Saddam may be interfering with more important American relationships, such as those with Russia, France, and China, as well as with Washington's Arab allies. Deterrence therefore accepts that the international anti-Iraq coalition—the foundation of the current containment policy—may be a thing of the past.

GOALS

The goal of deterrence is to send a clear message to Saddam Husayn that an Iraqi challenge to U.S. allies or interests will be met with a swift and intense U.S. military response, absent the hand-wringing and pin-pricks of previous showdowns. If Saddam Husayn commits an act of military aggression against the United States or its Gulf allies, or deploys or uses chemical or biological weapons, the United States will retaliate, first with overwhelming air power and then, if necessary, with a Desert Storm–style campaign. Just as important, this approach allows America's Arab allies to take the lead with regard to regional collective security and to do so with the confidence of a credible U.S. military response to Iraqi aggression. Deterrence assumes that any Iraqi military threat can be handled by U.S. military power, even if Iraq rebuilds its WMD programs. However, deterrence also argues that these goals should be the only goals of U.S. policy, and that efforts to continue to keep Iraq weak, or to remove Saddam from power, are unneccessary and counterproductive.

DESCRIPTION OF THE POLICY

Deterrence requires the following modifications to the current containment strategy:

- Accepting that Saddam Husayn is likely to remain in power, that efforts at undermining his regime are futile and divisive, and that UN sanctions against Iraq are unlikely to be sustained.
- Deemphasizing Iraq as a foreign policy issue with Washington's UN Security Council allies, and placing it instead in the context of global nonproliferation strategy.
- Encouraging more sustainable regional security arrangements.
- Deterring Iraq with a clear and credible U.S. military commitment.

These four components of an Iraq policy grounded in deterrence allow Washington to acknowledge the strategic realities of its situation with Iraq and regain the initiative in its regional policies.

Living with Saddam Husayn?

Deterrence accepts the tough reality that Saddam Husayn is likely to remain in power for the forseeable future and that, realistically, there is little the United States can do about it. Whereas the United States should not excuse the Iraqi dictator's crimes against his people, this position argues that it is Iraq's behavior beyond its borders, rather than within Iraq, that is the real concern of U.S. foreign policy.

Sanctions fatigue among Arab and UN allies also signals a likely end to UN sanctions on Iraq. Baghdad is already back in the oil business in a big way, as UN Security Council Resolution 1153 permits Iraq to sell more oil than it is currently capable of exporting.

Furthermore, a deterrence approach posits that the Iraqi military threat has been exaggerated, and that living with Saddam is about living with an Iraqi military threat that the United States should be able to handle indefinitely. According to this view, Iraq's conventional forces are in tatters and global proliferation controls are sufficient to manage the threat of Iraqi proliferation. Also, a strong and credible U.S. military deterrent posture should forestall any Iraqi military provocation for the foreseeable future.

As much as America's Arab allies may loathe and fear Saddam Husayn's regime, when push comes to shove, few would support a U.S.-brokered insurgency led by an organization like the Iraq National Congress (INC), which has little credibility among Iraqis either inside or outside Iraq, or for that matter among Arab governments. The precedent of such heavy-handed U.S. intervention would not sit well with many of Washington's friends and allies in the Arab world. Furthermore, many Arab states and Turkey might well express concern about the destabilizing effects of an Iraqi civil war, including the possibilities of Iranian intervention and Kurdish secession.

Deterrence does not necessarily argue for either recognizing or doing business with Saddam Husayn's Iraq. It merely shifts the focus of U.S. policy away from Washington's frustration and obsession with Iraq's dictator to Iraq's behavior outside its borders, which, it is argued, the United States can influence through a deterrent posture. Yet, the United States, along with its allies, might consider a limited form of engagement with Iraq to encourage and reinforce positive Iraqi behavior on terrorism, weapons of mass destruction (WMDs), human rights, the Arab–Israeli peace process, and Kuwaiti borders and prisoners of war (POWs).

Deemphasizing Iraq

Deterrence policy advocates deemphasizing Iraq as an issue in U.S. foreign policy with America's Security Council allies. This does not mean that Iraq should be taken off the U.S. foreign policy agenda at the United Nations. Rather, deterrence seeks to end Iraqi exceptionalism by placing it in the context of U.S. global arms proliferation concerns. According to this view, the Iraqi threat to U.S. interests has been exaggerated and, in the future, could become a detriment to Washngton's relations with Moscow, Paris, and Beijing.

The latest crisis revealed that Iraq has become a complicating issue in America's relations with Russia, France, and China, three countries with which the United States has significant global interests beyond Iraq. The incentives for them to break with the United States on Iraq are potentially strong enough that Washington may be able to maintain the international coalition only with dramatic tradeoffs in other foreign policy areas, if it can maintain it at all. Assuming both reasonable Iraqi compliance under the inspections regime of the UN Special Commission on Iraq (UNSCOM) and the absence of Iraqi mischief (neither safe assumptions, of course), these three countries could favor the lifting of sanctions in October 1998 or shortly thereafter.

Rather than continuing to fight an uphill and ultimately losing battle, a deterrent posture advocates that U.S. diplomacy should deal with Iraq in the context of its global arms proliferation concerns and strategies. Anticipating the eventual end of UN sanctions and intrusive UNSCOM inspections, deterrence proposes that the United States should deal with Iraq in the context of existing international agreements regarding proliferation, such as the Wassenauer Agreement, the Nuclear Non-Proliferation Treaty (NPT), the Chemical Weapons and Biological Weapons Conventions (CWC and BWC), and others, as the bases for managing Iraqi proliferation and WMD procurement. This would put an end to Iraqi exceptionalism in U.S. foreign policy while maintaining a rightful focus on the global concern of the United States and its allies regarding WMD proliferation, especially nuclear weapons.

The United States might also encourage measures similar to those of the Conventional Forces in Europe (CFE) agreement, for example, to monitor Iraq's conventional military strength. According to deterrence, if Saddam Husayn wants to waste his money rebuilding and restocking his obsolete conventional capabilities, U.S. military planners need not lose excessive sleep over it.

Under the current containment policy, the United States is insisting on the maintenance and expansion of UNSCOM and International Atomic Energy Agency (IAEA) inspections inside Iraq indefinitely. A deterrence posture, however, would acknowledge that the days of UN sanctions and intrusive UNSCOM inspections may be numbered and that it is not in Washington's interest to get drawn every few months into credibility-draining showdowns at Saddam Husayn's initiative.

Regional Security

Regional collective security is the real unfinished business of the Gulf War. After the American victory over Iraq in 1991, the United States marshaled its weighty political and military power to launch the Madrid process for Arab–Israeli peace, leaving behind the issues of Gulf security—in particular, what to do about Iraq and Iran, the reasons for America's military engagements in the Persian Gulf since 1987. One approach to regional security would be for the United States to consider resurrecting efforts to create a regional balance of power, playing a more moderate Iran against Iraq.

Another option would be for the United States to broker collective security arrangements among its Arab allies and Iran, with the understanding that the United States will support their efforts with a credible and swift military response should Iraq commit an act of aggression against Kuwait or Saudi Arabia. Regional collective security arrangements might institute a system of rewards and punishments either to isolate or to assimilate Iraq within the regional order. Engagement with Iraq could be used as a means to reward responsible Iraqi behavior regarding Kuwaiti sovereignty, the Arab–Israeli peace process, and international terrorism. Iraqi concessions in these areas could be reinforced by gradually allowing Iraq a larger say in regional affairs.

This approach would end the rather embarrassing theater of Washington's foreign policy elite regularly lecturing America's regional allies on the danger they face from Saddam Husayn's Iraq. Absent another Iraqi attack on its neighbors, the United States simply cannot win the so-called "propaganda war" against Iraq necessary to sustain containment or to enact a more proactive anti-Saddam policy. American policymakers do not seem to comprehend the extent of bitterness and frustration throughout the Arab world regarding U.S. policy toward Iraq. Many Arabs do not understand why the Iraqi people should suffer even more because of U.S. policy. Deterrence would allow the United States to remove this problem in its relationships with its Arab allies.

A Credible Military Deterrent

Deterrence means that the United States will respond swiftly with disproportionate military force should Iraq threaten American allies or interests with military force or terrorism, or if it deploys weapons of mass destruction. The U.S. response would be especially severe should Iraq use WMDs. The deterrence posture should be designed to demonstrate that the United States can and will handle any Iraqi military provocation, certainly with air power, and if necessary with ground forces.

Deterrence requires a leaner and meaner U.S. military presence in the Persian Gulf. The most appropriate means of carrying out deterrence would be a return to an "over the horizon" U.S. military presence, including a tripwire military force in Kuwait, combined with regular training exercises involving ground troops and appropriate air forces. These periodic exercises would reassure America's regional allies and signal the

U.S. commitment and capability to deter Iraqi aggression. The United States should be prepared, on short notice, to deliver a massive and sustained aerial bombardment of key sites in Iraq should Saddam Husayn cross Iraq's borders.

Targets should be those the Iraqi regime considers vital to its power base: the presidential palaces; arms production and possible dual-use facilities; Republican Guard and intelligence installations; and radio, television, and telecommunications transmitters. The presidential palaces may not contain any WMDs, but they would still be important because they are closely associated with Saddam Husayn. Likewise, the media and telecommunications capabilities are the means with which the regime communicates with its people. Cutting off the state-run radio and television during an attack would create the sense that the government has lost control and would perhaps send a signal to those inside that the time is at hand to move against the government. Such an attack, especially on short notice, would be a terrifying prospect for Saddam Husayn's regime. The importance of other potential military targets are described in detail elsewhere in this study and will not be recounted here.

If Saddam Husayn feels that he can get away with a quick land grab while the United States marshals its forces, deterrence fails. The point of this policy is as its name implies: to make so clear the U.S. determination and ability for massive military response that it deters Iraq from attacking its neighbors. A repetition of the so-called "Baker Ultimatum" regarding the assured American response to any Iraqi use of biological or chemical weapons against U.S. forces might also be an important component of a credible deterrent posture.

The United States should be prepared to act unilaterally under deterrence and not seek allied consensus or UN support for a military attack. Great Britain, for example, or other U.S. allies may wish to endorse deterrence and support American initiatives. The United States should of course welcome support for its policies from any quarter. Deterrence assumes that America's Gulf allies, especially Kuwait and Saudi Arabia, and Turkey will continue to provide the same forward basing rights and military cooperation that currently exists, as U.S. military power is there to be used solely in the case of Iraqi aggression against America's friends. Other than these forward bases, U.S. military forces would be reduced to a tripwire force in Kuwait, regular naval patrols, and a posture that is generally "over-the-horizon." Washington's Arab allies should welcome the otherwise reduced U.S. military presence and the absence of the divisive U.S. crisis diplomacy and rhetoric that have characterized past U.S.–Iraq showdowns. It should certainly be easier for them to justify to their citizens a U.S. military presence to defend their borders against an Iraqi attack, rather than to offer justice on American terms for Iraq's violations of its UN obligations.

The unilateral aspect of the assured U.S. military response, in the context of these clearly stated "red lines" regarding Iraqi provocation, should strengthen the American position. Saddam Husayn should have no doubt about what he should not do, nor about what the United States would do if he does.

END STATE

Deterrence argues for deemphasizing Iraq as a threat in U.S. foreign policy, transferring a substantial share of the responsiblity for collective security to America's regional allies, and responding to violations of clearly defined "red lines" with the nearly automatic use of military force. This policy would allow Washington to remove Iraq as a divisive issue with its UN and Arab allies, and end the frustrating game of challenge-and-response with Saddam Husayn. The desired result of deterrence would be an Iraq that accepts the American "red lines" and deals with its neighbors in a less threatening manner.

Putting Iraq in Perspective

ADVANTAGES

Pursuing a policy of deterrence would allow Washington to reap the following benefits:

- *Regain the initiative in its Iraq policy.* Containment is a basically defensive, reactive policy that grants the initiative to Saddam Husayn and thereby allows him to provoke periodic crises that have, in the past, worked to undermine American credibility. Deterrence provides Iraq with clear guidelines about what is acceptable and what is unacceptable behavior, from a U.S. perspective. In other words, the United States would redefine the rules in a way that more accurately reflects a cool calculation of U.S. interests. Under deterrence, the Iraqi dictator should have no doubt about the consequences of his actions. A U.S. military response to Iraqi aggression would require no UN or allied consensus, and it need not be "proportional." The unilateral nature of the U.S. military threat should make it both more threatening and more credible.

- *Remove Iraq as a divisive issue among its UN allies.* Iraq is becoming an increasingly divisive issue among America's allies, and putting it aside by pursuing deterrence provides a way of ending the frantic and enervating UN diplomacy that accompanies every Iraqi challenge to UNSCOM.

- *Remove Iraq as a divisive issue among its Arab allies.* Washington's policy toward Iraq is a source of tension in its relationships in the Arab world. Deterrence allows the United States to reduce the destabilizing effect of the large U.S. military presence in the region and to end the regional public relations disaster that accompanies U.S. support for sanctions on Iraq. From a "systemic" approach to Middle East politics, an indigenous collective security regime might, over the long run, contribute to greater stability.

- *Encourage Iraqi concessions.* By shifting from containment to deterrence, the United States could and should expect Iraqi concessions on other issues of concern to U.S. policy in the Middle East, such as terrorism, WMDs, the Arab–Israeli peace process, human rights, and Kuwaiti sovereignty and POWs. The regional approach to collective security described above could provide the framework for either isolating or assimilating Iraq, based upon Iraqi behavior in these and other areas.

- *Ditch the INC opposition option.* Deterrence agues for discouraging U.S. support for the INC as a viable alternative Iraqi government-in-exile. Despite protestations to the contrary, the reality is that six years after its formation, the INC is much worse off—especially without the support of Iraq's two main Kurdish opposition groups, the KDP and the Patriotic Union of Kurdistan (PUK)—at a time when Saddam Husayn appears to be stronger than at any time since the Gulf War. The INC also has yet to demonstrate its ability to galvanize support among independent Iraqis and other opposition groups, especially those inside non-Kurdish Iraq. Although INC president Ahmed Chalabi has succeeded in winning the hearts and minds of some in Washington, support for the INC runs much deeper along the Potomac than it does along the Tigris. In sum, U.S. support for the INC as "the" legitimate Iraqi opposition force represents a misguided policy that has little realistic chance of affecting developments inside Iraq.

- *Reducing the attention given Saddam in domestic politics.* American policymakers and citizens are understandably frustrated with Saddam Husayn. Deterrence would take Iraq off the radar screen of American politics unless Saddam Husayn commits another act of aggression or terror beyond his borders. With this approach, the U.S. government does not set itself up for successive Iraq-induced crises, during which attention is directed at the continuing rule in Baghdad of a man whom U.S. officials have compared to Hitler.

• *Cut costs.* Much ado is made about the costs of the U.S. military forces currently in the Persian Gulf and the greater costs of a more proactive anti-Saddam Husayn policy. Keeping watch over the no-fly zones costs approximately $680 million per year, and the "unanticipated" costs of increasing U.S. military presence during the last crisis has been estimated at $1.36 billion. Deterrence, on the other hand, requires a reduced military presence—a leaner and meaner commitment to military security.

• *Lower oil prices.* The return of Iraqi oil to the world market, during a period of supply glut and already low prices, could mean even lower energy prices, a clear benefit to the U.S. economy. Iraq could also open up to investment by U.S. companies.

LIABILITIES AND RISKS

Despite the advantages of deterrence listed above, the policy would maintain certain aspects of the status quo that may be unacceptable to Washington.

• *America and the world will have to continue to live with Saddam Husayn.* Under deterrence, the Iraqi dictator and the nature of his regime are discounted to emphasize the primacy of Iraqi "behavior" in U.S. foreign policy calculations. Yet, one of the assumptions of containment—that Saddam Husayn is "irredeemable" because of both his track record inside Iraq and his aggressions against Iran and Kuwait—still rings true. The end of containment would also probably be perceived throughout the Arab world and elsewhere as a victory by Iraq and an admission of defeat by the United States. This development could embolden the Iraqi dictator's regional ambitions. His behavior over the past seven years certainly gives few indications that either he or his regime is capable of playing a constructive role in

Iraqi or regional politics. Saddam Husayn has also displayed a troubling propensity for miscalculation. He might try to circumvent the American red lines through terror or subversion. His record of concealment, deception, and obfuscation with UNSCOM betrays the value he places on his WMD programs. Rebuilding those programs would be easier for him under deterrence.

- *Deterrence could possibly send the wrong signals.* Other would-be challengers to U.S. interests are obviously closely following U.S. policy toward Iraq. Some might view deterrence as betraying a lack of American will, revealing that the United States can be outlasted if its adversaries merely stay the course. This move could damage America's policy in Bosnia, for example. The U.S. return to an over-the-horizon posture might also be interpreted as a prelude to an American withdrawal from the Gulf, as Great Britain did in 1971.

- *Iraq would remain a domestic issue.* Any U.S. president that backs down from a faceoff with Saddam Husayn has to worry that this issue will haunt him later. Some Republicans have already used the Iraq issue as a means of attacking Bill Clinton's foreign policy. If this president or the next were to announce a shift to deterrence, he or she should be prepared for withering criticism. A drawdown of U.S. forces in the Gulf might also embolden isolationist tendencies in the United States, complicating the use of U.S. military force in the Gulf should deterrence fail. The possible lack of UN or international support for military action against Iraq could also erode public support for an American military strike, in the event that it is needed.

- *Deterrence could erode containment.* The containment regime, while imperfect, has otherwise proved quite effective in keeping tabs on Iraq's WMD programs. By deemphasizing Iraq, the United States might have difficulty maintaining three components of the current containment strategy: the UNSCOM inspections and monitoring regime inside Iraq; U.S. overflights of Iraqi territory; and restrictions on the sale of military and dual-use technology to Iraq. These remnants of containment might be accepted by Iraq as necessary tradeoffs for the lifting of sanctions, but they would certainly be more difficult to maintain under deterrence than under some forms of containment.

- *Irresponsible behavior by U.S. allies may be encouraged.* Even under containment and tight UN sanctions, Russia provided Iraq with sophisticated gyroscopes for intercontinental ballistic missiles. One could assume that if or when sanctions are lifted, sensitive dual-use weapons technology will quickly find its way into Iraq. Russia and France had profitable military and economic relations with Saddam Husayn's government prior to the Gulf War and, given their long-standing strategic interests in Iraq, it is easy to see how these ties might be resumed, albeit gradually, as the United States deemphasizes Iraq in its foreign policy.
- *Regional powers could appease and accommodate Iraq.* Regional collective security is a worthy ideal, but in the real world, power rules, and Iraq still is much more powerful than its Arab neighbors. The Gulf Cooperation Council (GCC) states have always been wary of an Iraqi role in regional security. Collective security in the Persian Gulf is only a possibility if the United States brokers the deal, and any such deal would be unlikely as long as Saddam Husayn rules Iraq.
- *America may abdicate its moral obligation.* The United States should shoulder some moral obligation to hold Saddam Husayn and his regime accountable for crimes against the Iraqi people and those committed against Iran and Kuwait during both Gulf wars. Deterrence allows little

room for moral argument.

- *Iraq could reassert its oil power.* Certainly, prices may decrease in the short run, but the reemergence of Iraqi oil power would equip Saddam Husayn with a powerful foreign policy tool, one that he used effectively to increase oil prices in July 1990. An increased Iraqi role in OPEC is not necessarily a positive development for Iraq's relations with Kuwait, Saudi Arabia, and the United Arab Emirates. Furthermore, the reconstruction and development of Iraq's oil industry will provide even more powerful economic incentives for French, Russian, Chinese and other oil companies to resume business with Iraq. Inevitably, American oil companies and businesses would also want in on the action, creating a potentially powerful lobby for engagement with Iraq.
- *Iraq would remain an international issue.* The latest crisis revealed that Iraq poses the greatest challenge to U.S. policy in the Middle East. Saddam Husayn himself recognizes that Iraq is an international issue that cannot be localized. Indeed, "the battle for Iraq" is the most significant strategic contest in the Middle East, the results of which will define the strategic landscape of the region for the next decade and beyond.

CONCLUSIONS

Deterrence reflects the difficult reality that the current containment regime may not be sustainable and that Saddam Husayn might just outlast another American president or two. Sanctions fatigue among America's UN and Arab allies will in all likelihood grow, thereby increasing Washington's isolation both in the Security Council and in the Middle East. In that context, a more clearly defined articulation of U.S. interests regarding Iraqi behavior, buttressed by a regional security regime and a credible U.S. military deterrent, offers a realistic means of dealing with Iraq. On the other hand, deterrence runs the risk of a Saddam Husayn whose behavior may not be constrained in any meaningful way until he crosses his border. Deterrence requires the United States to trust that it will have not only the political will and military strength to stop him if he again attacks his neighbors, but also the ability to ignore his other atrocities and machinations.

Chapter 5

INVADE
Conquering and Occupying Iraq

John Hillen

The principal difference between this policy option and previous ones is that this is the only option in which the United States itself is the prime determinant of the outcome. Invading and occupying Iraq represents *an imposed solution, not a negotiated one*. The other options outlined in this book have their relative merits and risks, but all rely for success on many other actors (including Saddam Husayn himself) whom the United States does not necessarily control or influence. Conversely, having U.S. and allied forces invade and occupy Iraq and oust Saddam Husayn removes the Iraqi president and his Ba'th regime from decisions about Iraq's future and puts the United States and its allies firmly in control of the immediate outcome.

Obviously, the United States and its allies would never entertain such an extreme policy unless Iraq carried out a significant act of aggression. Despite the latent threat that Saddam Husayn's regime poses to the Persian Gulf and Middle East, it is difficult to imagine a well-represented multinational coalition gearing up for an invasion of Iraq tomorrow. In the opinions of most in the international community, Saddam's current pattern of truculent behavior, however troublesome, would not warrant a war. It is quite a stretch to expect local and international support for an invasion of Iraq precipitated only by something like Saddam's tactic of aggravating the United Nations Special Commission on Iraq (UNSCOM) and obstructing its mission. Rather, an act that could trigger the response described here might include further aggression or bullying directed at Kuwait or Saudi Arabia, the sponsoring of spectacular terrorist acts against the United States or its citizens, the violent repression of Kurdish or Shi'i minorities within Iraq (especially if done with chemical or biological agents, as in the past), or the deployment of a significant weapons of mass destruction (WMD) program flagrantly violating the UN Security Council resolutions banning Iraqi WMD.

An unprovoked act of Iraqi aggression, as that against Kuwait in 1990, would allow the United States and its allies to mobilize the domestic and international support necessary to undertake this complex, expensive, and arduous operation. Even so, such an undertaking is not without great costs, much diplomatic and military labor, and huge potential risks. Eliminating Saddam and his regime, as well as overseeing the accession of a new Iraqi government, would take away the uncertainty associated with the other options but replace that with an expensive certainty. "Doing the job" and "going all the way" make clear the outcome and who will decide it, but they raise the geopolitical stakes and associated risks considerably. The rewards are evident and, to some degree, even assured (certainly the United States could not afford to fail after implementing this policy), but they could not be achieved without tremendous effort and the possibility of serious downsides.

THE GOAL

During the latest crisis with Iraq, U.S. policy focused on the symptoms (WMDs) and not the problem (Saddam Husayn's regime). As such, the most likely targets for U.S. military action during the crisis of November 1997–February 1998 were sites that made or hid WMDs. This policy reverses those objectives. The target of this policy is that which causes the threat: Saddam Husayn and his regime. The goal of this policy is to remove Saddam Husayn and his Ba'th party from power in Iraq and install an Iraqi government pledged to international norms and a peaceful coexistence with its neighbors. It is assumed that Saddam Husayn and the Iraqi military will resist this goal, which must therefore be accomplished through coercion in general and the offensive use of U.S. and allied military forces in particular.

DESCRIPTION OF THE POLICY

A campaign to invade and occupy Iraq could take many different forms and vary greatly in its military execution depending on the circumstances. Yet, any campaign should follow these principles:

- *The campaign must enjoy international support.* Naturally, the more international support the better, but a minimum level of military cooperation and political acquiescence from other powers in the international arena would be necessary to carry out this operation. Much of the support could be passive or take the form of no active opposition.

- *The campaign must be actively supported by key allies in the region.* This is a political and military *sine qua non* for many different reasons. Local support such as that shown during Desert Storm would ease diplomatic and military concerns considerably. If a similar effort is not forthcoming, a minimum level of active support from allies in the region is required to undertake even the smallest and most hopeful operation aimed at replacing the current Iraqi regime.

- *The campaign must have congressional and U.S. public support.* Without support from Capitol Hill or the American public, the flexibility and staying power of this campaign to invade and occupy Iraq would be severely limited. Casualties or controversy in such a serious and taxing military operation could not be overcome if the mission had limited domestic support.

- *Military goals must be linked conclusively to political goals such that accomplishing the former entails achieving the latter.* The military and political goals should be clearly defined, measurable, decisive, attainable, and sustainable. The objectives of the battlefield commanders, at both the tactical and operational levels, should be tied clearly to the strategic and political goals of the campaign. If this link is unclear, battlefield successes could be irrelevant to the ultimate outcome, or military losses could be inconsequential and incurred in vain.

• *Although the U.S. military will depose the regime and maintain security and order afterwards, Iraqi opposition leaders and an international transition authority must take the lead in organizing a viable Iraqi government.* The United States should not spend decades occupying and reinventing Iraq as it did in Germany and Japan after World War II. Nor should it quit the country soon after unseating Saddam. The U.S. military will bolster the occupation of Iraq for some time, but ultimately the Iraqi people must be charged with the task of forming an effective Iraqi government. In this they will have assistance from an international transition authority, regional organizations, and the United States.

International Support

A U.S.-led coalition seeking to invade and occupy Iraq would profit enormously from broad international support. That being said, such support could be organized in several different ways to ensure that it is sufficiently broad and deep to pay very real political and military dividends, but not so deep that it makes for a war run by committee. The logical place to organize such high level support is through the UN Security Council. As with Korea in 1950 and Kuwait in 1990, U.S.-sponsored resolutions passed by the UN Security Council can be an important base of legitimacy in the eyes of international and domestic political communities. A U.S.-led coalition invading Iraq would gain from the political blessing of the Security Council, even as it keeps the UN itself outside of the strategic management of the campaign. It should be stressed however, that while Security Council approval would be preferable, it is not absolutely essential. Neither international nor American law requires a UN resolution to undertake the invasion and occupation of another country in the event that it is a response (as can be assumed) to unprovoked aggression by that country. International legitimacy for coalition actions would most likely be based on Article 51 of the UN Charter—the right to individual and collective self-defense. In such a case the UN need not be involved in legitimizing or setting coalition goals. Nonetheless, the United States and other members of the coalition would certainly seek to work through the UN in this instance—especially as they have done so in all dealings with Iraq over the past eight years. A well-supported UN Security Council resolution authorizing the actions of the campaign would be a tremendous advantage for mobilizing international and domestic support for the U.S.-led actions that would follow in Iraq. In addition, a resolution denouncing or even indicting Saddam Husayn himself would have the effect of isolating Saddam further from the rest of Iraq or other international supporters. A clear expression of support, such as that provided by Resolution 678 authorizing Desert Storm, would be infinitely better.

Outside of the role of regional partners, certain allies can be counted upon to support U.S. actions regardless of the variables mentioned above. Others will come to the table based upon either the nature of the Iraqi aggression or the strength of the international resolutions supporting the coalition's invasion of Iraq. In any case, whereas the military participation of local allies can be critical (as outlined below), few non–Persian Gulf allies other than Britain are important for military success. Indeed, many, if not the majority, of military contingents in the thirty-one-member Desert Storm coalition were militarily irrelevant to the campaign. They were, however, of great political utility, as they proved how broad-based the coalition was. Yet, for many different reasons, only U.S. and British troops engaged the Republican Guard, and only U.S. and British warships operated in the northern Persian Gulf. More than ten other nations participated in the air attacks, but together they constituted less than 10 percent of coalition air sorties and conducted almost no missions that were at the centerpiece of that campaign. That imbalance would likely continue in this campaign. Therefore, the recruitment of a broad military coalition would once again be of political value, but the absence of some global partners would not be a "show stopper" militarily.

Active Regional Assistance

SAUDI ARABIA. As in Desert Storm, Saudi Arabia would be the indispensable coalition partner, for political and military reasons. Militarily, there is simply no escaping the need for Saudi bases, port facilities, logistics sites, and transportation infrastructure. In the event of significant and threatening Iraqi aggression and a serious American commitment to a decisive campaign, support should be forthcoming from the Saudis (as it was during Desert Storm). If Saudi support is present but circumscribed, it is still possible to launch the campaign against Iraq. In such a case, "passive" Saudi support would still have to include two items. The first is the use of Saudi airfields for all coalition aircraft, to include strike aircraft. More than 1,000 aircraft were based at eleven or more Saudi airbases during Desert Storm. A similar capability would be needed. It would be possible to base strike aircraft elsewhere, but at a significant cost in the effectiveness of a coalition air campaign.

The second element of Saudi support would have to be the use of Saudi port facilities, logistics sites, and transportation hubs for the deployment and supply of air, ground, and sea forces. A main or supporting attack launched from Saudi Arabia would dramatically increase the effectiveness of a two-pronged ground assault toward Baghdad (see map and concept of operations below), but the southern portion of the ground campaign could be launched from Kuwait alone if necessary. As with restrictions on the use of air bases, reliance on Kuwait alone would involve a commensurate increase in operational complications and a drop-off in effectiveness. Politically, Saudi Arabia is also indispensable. Riyadh carries tremendous political weight in Arab councils, especially among its smaller Gulf brethren. In particular, the Saudis will have to make the case for the operation to the Arab world and the Islamic *umma*. The Saudis likewise will prove extremely important in garnering support both in Europe and Asia. Furthermore, Washington may require Saudi financial assistance to defray the costs of the invasion, to provide inexpensive oil to Jordan, and otherwise to guarantee that an invasion will not be allowed to disrupt the oil market too seriously. Finally, and perhaps of greatest importance: If Saudi Arabia is not on board with the operation—at least passively—the United States is unlikely to find many other Arab or European states willing to sign on.

KUWAIT. Although it may be possible to undertake this operation with only passive support from Saudi Arabia and some other regional allies, Kuwait must be actively involved. In other words, for the invasion and occupation of Iraq to succeed, Kuwait must allow the coalition to launch ground and air assaults against Iraq from its territory and continue to be the main base of coalition operations during the campaign. Nonetheless, Kuwait's political, financial, and moral support might ultimately outweigh its military utility for a campaign of this size. The country's military basing capability and relevant infrastructure are important, but they pale in comparison to what is available from Saudi Arabia or even other Gulf states. In addition, concentrating all or a substantial portion of the coalition's offensive capability in one relatively small country is poor security planning and invites attack. Offensive military assets should be dispersed for protection and massed only at the point of attack. Military considerations aside, it is hard to imagine how the United States could put together the necessary diplomatic support for an invasion without active Kuwaiti participation. Given the immediacy of the Iraqi threat, Kuwait is the country most likely to support a forcible invasion and occupation of Iraq. If Kuwait is unwilling to participate, few other nations are likely to believe it in their interests to do so.

TURKEY. Like Saudi Arabia, Turkey is a country whose active participation would greatly increase the effectiveness of the campaign but whose passive support could be enough to undertake the operation. Of particular importance are Turkish airbases, such as Incirlik. Incirlik continues to host more than fifty allied aircraft patrolling the no-fly zone over northern Iraq, so it is a fair assumption that Turkey would at least continue this sort of policy for an invasion. It is important, though, that Turkey play a more active role. It is quite possible that Saddam and his Republican Guard would move north to avoid a direct battle with coalition forces closing on Baghdad. In this case, as seen below in the concept of operations, a blocking position of sorts would be established, principally from the air, in northern Iraq. Although coalition air forces undertaking this operation would also come from aircraft carriers or bases in Crete, mainland Greece, and Italy (as they did in Desert Storm), Turkey's support would be greatly needed. In addition, northern Iraq will be a theater heavily invested by coalition special operations forces and possibly more ground troops. Turkey's support of these forces, as during Operation Provide Comfort, would be required.

Moreover, Turkey's pledge of noninterference in the occupation phase of the campaign would be critical, as the coalition will plan to turn all of Iraq over to a new Iraqi government, not one riven with factional disputes or interference by neighbors. **EGYPT.** Egypt's active participation in an invasion and occupation of Iraq would be extremely useful in lending the appropriate pan-Arab and Islamic veneer to the operation. Failing that, Egypt's passive participation is vital. The United States must have overflight rights across Egyptian airspace and unimpeded transit through the Suez Canal to deploy and sustain an invasion force in the Gulf. The alternatives—flying across Israel and Jordan, and sailing from the Pacific or around Africa—would place an enormous political and logistical strain on the entire operation. It would also be very helpful for U.S. aircraft flying to the Gulf to be able to land at Egyptian airfields when necessary, and for U.S. combat units to use Egyptian territory for maneuvers and exercises preparatory to an invasion.

IRAN. If a sympathetic Iranian government wanted to provide assistance, so much the better, but the critical requirement is merely to prevent Tehran's active opposition. Iranian domestic politics is in considerable flux at the moment and it is impossible to know who will hold power in Tehran at the time of a U.S.-led invasion of Iraq. A reformist government might actually be willing to aid the invasion, but a hardline government would likely prove quite hostile to the idea of the United States removing the government of another Persian Gulf state and installing a regime more palatable to Washington. If Iran wanted to interfere with an invasion of Iraq, it could prove very problematic: Even without opening hostilities, Iranian military activity could force the United States to divert considerable assets to guard against Iranian naval and air strikes along the length of the Persian Gulf. Likewise, Iranian troops could infiltrate Iraq as "volunteers" to help thwart the ground assault. Consequently, it is essential that Iran simply be kept neutral throughout the course of the operation, especially, as with Turkey, during the occupation phase.

ISRAEL. As in the Gulf War, Israel's most important role would be to remain on the sidelines. Israeli participation could only complicate an invasion of Iraq. Nevertheless, such an effort might be even more difficult this time than in 1991. The Israelis have repeatedly warned that they believe their failure to respond to Iraqi Scud missile attacks during the Gulf War weakened the credibility of their deterrent. Moreover, in the event of a U.S.-led invasion designed to overturn the regime, Saddam might actually employ weapons of mass destruction against Israel, either to try to bring Jerusalem into the conflict (as he tried in 1991) or out of simple vengeance.

JORDAN. Jordan falls into the category of "nice to have" as an ally, as far as coalition planning is concerned. In particular, in the event that Saddam does attempt to launch missiles at Israel from Iraq's western desert, Scud-hunting air and ground missions would be more effective if conducted from Jordan. Because King Hussein refused to join the allied coalition against Saddam in the Gulf War, if he could be persuaded to support an invasion of Iraq, this would be a considerable diplomatic coup for the United States. On the other hand, if Jordan abstained altogether, it would not hurt the invasion either militarily or diplomatically.

OTHER GULF STATES. During Operation Desert Storm, coalition air forces used a dozen bases in Qatar, Bahrain, Oman, and the United Arab Emirates. In addition, Bahrain now supports the headquarters of the U.S. Navy's Fifth Fleet and Qatar is home to a U.S. armored brigade's pre-positioned equipment. The active participation of at least most of these states in this campaign would be necessary, especially if Saudi Arabia were to place restrictions on its support.

OTHER ARAB STATES. As in 1991, it would be politically useful to include as many other Arab (and Islamic) states as possible in the coalition to invade Iraq. With Saudi Arabia and Egypt lending at least passive support, this participation would be neither essential nor difficult to get.

Congressional and U.S. Public Support

Since the end of World War II, the lines of responsibility between Congress, the president, and the American public have become blurred with regard to the support and/or authorization of military action. To ensure the necessary domestic political support, it would be ideal to proceed with this operation under the banner of a formal declaration of war. Yet, that may prove politically impossible, in which case the president must take other measures to ensure that he has the support of Congress and the American public before undertaking this campaign. A congressional vote of support for the U.S.-led invasion and occupation of Iraq is an absolute minimum—especially with the president activating hundreds of thousands of reservists and national guardsmen, as in Desert Storm. It is imperative that in this campaign, which promises to be of much greater duration than Desert Storm, Congress be fully supportive to the end. In addition, if the American public is convinced that the invasion is worthwhile and will be successful, it will support the effort despite the inevitable casualties. On the eve of Desert Storm, with some commentators predicting up to 10,000 casualties, many polls showed more than 80 percent of Americans supporting the effort. If the campaign is not supported, a few American casualties will be enough to foment damaging political discontent—as was the case in Somalia.

Clear Military Goals for the Invasion

The mission of the coalition forces will be to occupy all of Iraq, and to engage and defeat any and all Iraqi military forces that offer resistance. The military commander will accomplish this through a joint campaign of multinational air, sea, ground, and special operations forces that will strike Iraqi resistance throughout the depth and breadth of their defenses. The Republican Guard and Special Republican Guard units represent Saddam's "center of gravity" and will be the focus of the ground campaign. Initial coalition forces will move quickly to engage and destroy these units, bypassing other Iraqi forces to do so. Follow-on forces will suppress other Iraqi resistance, invest Baghdad, control and/or occupy the city, and ensure that Saddam Husayn and the Ba'th party leaders are captured, killed, or driven from Iraq and pursued by other means.

Concept of Operations

The invasion and occupation of Iraq will happen in four phases. At any time during these phases the objective could be achieved and Saddam Husayn's regime removed from power. That possibility should not preclude the occupation of Iraq and the transition to a new government. The phases are as follows:

Phase I—*Initial Deployment.* The first units arrive in the theater, beginning this phase. This phase ends with the start of the air campaign. *Estimated time:* Twenty-five to forty days after the announcement of the deployment.

Phase II—*Buildup and Air Attack.* The buildup of air, ground, and naval forces into the theater continues, and the initiative is maintained by beginning a strategic air campaign against Iraq. Targeting priorities would be centered on achieving command of the air, preventing Iraqi retaliation against the coalition buildup, and disrupting strategic command and control. Targets would be anti-aircraft systems, command-and-control centers and infrastructure, WMD sites, Scud launchers, the Iraqi Air Force and airbases, Republican Guard units moving to threaten neighbors or the coalition buildup, and Saddam Husayn himself. Special operations units would also be working in Iraq during this phase, especially in helping to organize Kurdish and Shi'i operations in support of coalition

FRIENDLY SITUATION

A campaign to invade and occupy cannot be launched quickly and requires months for a force buildup. A truly grave situation in the region could speed events, but ultimately the coalition will be limited by many logistical and transportation factors weighing on the movement of hundreds of thousands of troops and equipment to the region. While military planners often make estimates based on worst-case scenarios, the force structure and operational plan here is one that is neither best-case nor worst-case. This plan is a prudent estimate for coalition forces based on several assumptions: that the regular Iraqi Army is essentially irrelevant and mostly will not fight, that the Iraqi Air Force will be of no consequence, that large areas of Iraq will be friendly or at least passive to coalition forces (the Kurdish North and Shi'i South), and that the Republican Guard and other regime security forces will not defend Baghdad and other cities in a house-to-house campaign. It is reasonable to assume that during the campaign Iraq will give up Saddam or he will flee with a number of henchmen to Iran or elsewhere. Conversely, it is hard to imagine Baghdad digging in for a Stalingrad-like resistance in defense of Saddam. Thus, based on the U.S. military's doctrine for joint campaign planning and the current capabilities of Iraq's armed forces, the minimum coalition forces needed to undertake this plan and deal with some unanticipated setbacks along the way are:

GROUND FORCES:

MAIN ATTACK: 4 U.S. divisions (1 airborne, 1 air assault, 2 armored/mechanized)
1 U.S. armored cavalry regiment
2 U.S. Apache helicopter brigades
1–2 UK mechanized infantry brigades
RESERVE: 3–4 U.S. national guard armored/mechanized infantry brigades

Conquering and Occupying Iraq

SUPPORTING
ATTACK: 2 U.S. divisions (1 marine, 1 mechanized)
               1 U.S. armored cavalry regiment (light)
RESERVE: 3–4 U.S. National Guard armored/
                   mechanized infantry brigades

In addition to these main combat units, ground forces would include all the requisite support units. The combat units would also be reinforced by certain units whose capabilities particularly suited the campaign—multiple launch rocket system battalions for instance. Moreover, for this campaign, support units would be augmented by thousands of civil affairs and psychological operations specialists mobilized from the reserves. Whereas this is standard for most operations, those specialties would be in particular demand for the occupation phase of this campaign.

AIR FORCES: 8 tactical fighter wings (U.S.)
             1 tactical fighter wing (U.K)
             3–4 tactical fighter wings (Arab allies)
             400–450 support aircraft
NAVAL AND NAVAL
AIR FORCES: 4 carrier battle groups
             60+ warships total
TOTAL U.S. MILITARY PERSONNEL IN IRAQI THEATER:
             310,000–340,000

Along with the deployed forces specified here, hundreds of thousands of reservists in the United States would need to be mobilized to support military operations in the Iraq theater, Europe, the United States itself, and as part of contingency plans for unexpected scenarios. In Desert Storm, more than 200,000 reservists were activated with more than 100,000 serving in theater.

objectives. This phase ends with the beginning of the ground campaign. *Estimated Time:* Forty-five to ninety days.

Phase III—*Invasion.* This phase consists of the actual invasion of Iraq, defeat of the Republican Guard units, and capture of Baghdad (see map, next page). During this phase much of the air campaign will switch to targets directly impeding the ground invasion. The scheme of maneuver would center on a main attack and a supporting attack. One obvious strategy would be for the main attack, preferably launched from Saudi Arabia, to move quickly through unoccupied desert and approach Baghdad through the Karbala/al-Hillah area. Airborne and air assault units would move ahead of the ground forces on several different avenues to secure key terrain, bridges, and road crossings. Apache helicopters and close air support would protect the flanks of the main attack and reconnoiter forward. This maneuver will cause the Republican Guard divisions around Baghdad to move or mass, at which point coalition air forces will attack them. Coalition ground forces will engage the remnants on the ground. The supporting ground attack would move from Kuwait through Basra and up the Euphrates and Tigris valley.

The main attack would initially invest Baghdad and then move in pursuit of the remaining Republican Guard divisions. Surviving elements from around Baghdad will likely have fled northward. To prevent the Republican Guard divisions from fleeing into the mountains of northern Iraq, the coalition will have established, primarily through airpower, a blocking position along a line running from Mosul to Irbil to Karkuk. Airborne and air assault troops could reinforce this blocking position if necessary. The supporting attack, and the uncommitted reserves from both attacks, would occupy and control Baghdad as well as the other major population centers in coalition-occupied territory. Symbols of the regime would be destroyed. As with every phase, special operations, civil affairs, and psychological

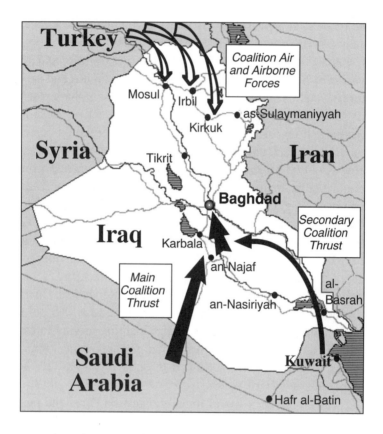

operations forces would be undertaking complex campaigns in support of the main coalition operations. They will especially work to gain the help of anti-Saddam Iraqis and to help ensure that Iraq's conscript forces do not fight. This phase ends when organized Iraqi resistance has ended. *Estimated Time:* Speculative, but twenty-five to seventy-five days is a fair guess.

Phase IV—*Occupation.* This phase starts with the end of organized Iraqi military resistance to coalition operations. In the event that there are no "wild-card" scenarios (biological or chemical weapons use, tough house-to-house defense of Baghdad), the United States can expect 3,000 to 4,000 casualties with perhaps 1,000 troops killed in action. This is an optimistic, but not unrealistic, prediction. Wild-card scenarios could change that forecast dramatically. During the years of the occupation, hundreds of troops could be killed because of isolated hostilities, pockets of resistance, and accidents.

Sustainable Iraqi Government

Once the military campaign is over, the next step is to ensure a smooth transition from the collapse of Saddam's regime to the formation of a functioning new Iraqi government. It is not intended that the United States and its coalition allies occupy Iraq for decades on the Germany or Japan model. Nor, as occurred recently in Haiti, will the United States quickly rebuild Iraq's political institutions, hand them over to new Iraqi leaders, and speedily exit the country. The participation of U.S. military forces in the occupation of Iraq should be long enough to protect the work of the international transitional authority and to promote the stability of the new Iraqi regime. It should, however, be short enough to reinforce the temporary nature of the American role in occupying Iraq and the responsibility of the new Iraqi government to govern effectively without support from foreign troops occupying the country. Even so, it is possible for the United States to become bogged down in the occupation of Iraq or for a new Iraqi government to fall apart soon after the occupation forces have left the country. The dilemma for policymakers is that the most certain way to ensure success in the mission is to stay for a long time—a situation not likely to be tolerated in the United States or the region.

Nonetheless, it should be possible to emplace an effective Iraqi government in a few years. The removal of Saddam and the Ba'th regime will not necessitate the complete turnover of the many systems that administered Iraq's public institutions. Not every Iraqi school teacher, military officer, bureaucrat, or official should be indicted and removed from office. Nor should every Iraqi resistance group be thrust into a governing position after the fall of the Ba'th regime. Rather, this occupation should be viewed along the lines of the French model in World War II, in which the collaborating Vichy regime was replaced with French republicans, only some of whom had gone underground or overseas to resist Hitler. The Ba'th regime will be removed, but few Iraqi elites have been so heavily vested in it that they could not be vigorous participants in a new Iraqi government. Several principles should underpin the objectives of the occupation:

- The coalition will preserve Iraq as a sovereign nation and not permit breakaway ethnic or religious states from what was Iraq.

- To the greatest extent possible, local Iraqi authorities should undertake the administration of the country and organization of the transition. Because most officials are connected with Saddam's regime, they should be screened, but they need not be rejected out of hand. The new government will need experienced Iraqi administrators and neither the coalition military forces nor the transitional authority should administer the country longer than necessary.

- That said, the coalition is legally and ethically responsible for the complete administration of Iraq after its occupation. The coalition's civil affairs units will take the lead, but it should work along with the transitional authority to encourage the transfer of administrative duties to Iraqi authorities.

- The transitional authority is the key element in the occupation and must have legitimacy, authority, and a realizable transition plan. The transitional authority can be sponsored by a regional organization such as the Arab League or by a broader international organization such as the UN. The transitional authority is a necessary phase of authority between the coalition's military forces and new Iraqi authorities.

The U.S. Occupation

As implied above, the occupation is a three-phase operation. In general, the U.S. military role and the number of U.S. troops in Iraq would gradually lessen with each phase. The roles of the U.S. military forces and other authorities are spelled out in some detail below. The general characteristics of each phase are as follows:

Phase I—*Initial occupation.* In this phase the coalition military forces constitute the governing authority in occupied Iraq. They will defend Iraq's territorial integrity, maintain public order, and be responsible for providing all services, some of which (such as education) may still be temporarily suspended as a result of the upheaval of the war. The official in charge will be the coalition military commander. In addition to maintaining a stable environment in and around Iraq, the U.S. military commander will oversee the rebuilding of Iraq's defense forces. Military police and military civil affairs units will take the lead in providing public security and the administration of basic services. This phase ends with the handover of authority to the international transitional authority. *Estimated time:* Three to nine months.

Phase II—*Transition to Iraqi Government.* In this phase the international transitional authority will be the governing power in Iraq, assisted in enforcing its authority by residual coalition forces. The authority, the link between the military occupation and the new Iraqi government, will work to rebuild Iraq's public institutions in stages. At each stage, the authority will identify measurable criteria in the transition from international to Iraqi rule. Areas in which the authority will operate include law enforcement agencies, the judiciary, public finance, public health, public works, utilities, transportation, education, and local government. In each of these areas, the authority will attempt to identify new Iraqi leaders, train them, and help them to rebuild the institutions of governance. As this phase draws to a close, the authority will turn over the administration of certain areas or the performance of certain functions to Iraqi officials. The official in charge will be the chief of the international transitional authority and he or she will be assisted by the coalition military commander. The authority itself will be the lead agency. This phase will end with Iraqi elections or the international recognition and certification of a new Iraqi government. *Estimated time:* Two to five years.

Phase III—*New Iraqi Government.* In this phase the new Iraqi government will be seated and the coalition forces begin their final withdrawal—although they should have been successively reducing force presence throughout the occupation. The international transitional authority can also institute a phased withdrawal in this stage. This phase ends when the authority cedes all governing powers to the sovereign government of Iraq. As noted, territorially this will be the same state of Iraq that the coalition invaded. The people of Iraq, through elections or force of arms, can later attempt to change the governance or make-up of Iraq as they desire.

Throughout these phases, U.S. military forces will be responsible primarily for the physical security and public order of Iraq itself. Not only must the U.S. military defend Iraq's borders, but it must also maintain internal security. It can be expected that various Iraqi factions (Kurdish groups, Shi'is, and others) will seek to take advantage of the power vacuum in Iraq to advance their positions. As with the Israeli occupation of southern Lebanon, this could challenge occupation authorities in several different ways, such as with sporadic outbreaks of violence, organized attacks on occupation forces, or full scale factional fighting. In addition, regional powers such as Iran and possibly Turkey or Jordan could seek to take advantage of the situation by paring off parts of Iraq. A robust U.S. military presence will have to guard against these possibilities. Furthermore, as noted, special operations forces, military police, and civil affairs units will bolster and help to rebuild the Iraqi military, police forces, and other public institutions before handing the responsibility for these tasks to the international transitional authority. The U.S. military will continue to support the work of the transitional authority once it is leading these efforts. During the first years of the occupation, as few as 150,000 U.S. troops and as many as 300,000 will be needed. If the situation is stable and progress is being made, they can be reduced dramatically in later years. These numbers are based on the U.S. military's joint civil affairs campaign planning doctrine and vary based on factors such as internal resistance, external threats, and political stability.

An International Transitional Authority

Transition away from occupation will have to be accomplished ad hoc by groups of diplomats, civil servants, law enforcement officials, public institution specialists, and other government officials. Either a regional organization or the UN can sponsor and organize the transitional authority. Similar types of authorities, albeit much smaller in scale, have been managed by NATO in Bosnia and by the UN in many different recent operations. The transitional authority will be the governing authority in Iraq between the periods of coalition military government and the new Iraqi government. The coalition's military forces will assist the authority in maintaining physical security and public order, but it should aim to return those tasks to Iraqi forces and the police as soon as these forces are able to resume control. Likewise, control of other public institutions should be returned to Iraqi officials as the institutions become viable and self-sustaining. The transitional authority will be a large and complex operation and, during initial stages, will most likely consist of at least 10,000 to 15,000 civilian officials.

The United States and the international transitional authority will rebuild a governmental system in Iraq. After decades of Saddam's totalitarian rule, this will not be an easy task. Most elites were either coopted by the system or else killed. Iraqis generally learned to be apolitical and few have any understanding of genuine political leadership. Consequently, it may be necessary for the occupying powers and the international transitional authority to create a new Iraqi government gradually, beginning with local-level political bodies, and then slowly building provincial-level governments, before establishing a new national-level government.

Upon being certified by the transitional authority and recognized by the international community, the new Iraqi government will assume all responsibilities for the territorial integrity of Iraq and the welfare of the Iraqi people. If geopolitical conditions warrant, the United States or regional partners could conclude a treaty of assistance with the new Iraqi government that would guarantee aid if the new regime is threatened from within or from outside powers.

Diplomatic Considerations

The occupation of Iraq and creation of a new Iraqi regime could prove the most problematic and taxing aspect of the entire campaign because Iraq's neighbors, and other states in the region, will want to shape the new regime to suit their preferences. Iraq's oil wealth, population, natural resources, and crucial geostrategic position on the Middle Eastern map make it a key factor in the calculations of every regional government. Who rules in Iraq is therefore a paramount concern of many states.

A key task of the United States during the occupation phase would be to circumvent efforts by the regional states to cajole, wheedle, and intrigue for a new Iraqi government most favorable to themselves. All will undoubtedly support individual Iraqi personalities predisposed to their own interests. In addition, each state will have specific goals it will try to realize in forming a new Iraqi government:

TURKEY will seek to ensure first that the Iraqi Kurds do not receive any special status, second that the new regime in Baghdad will help Ankara to deal with Kurdistan Workers' Party (PKK) operations from Iraqi territory, and third that Turkey retains its privileged status as a conduit for the export of Iraqi oil. Turkey will also want a strong, centralized regime in Baghdad, not only to guarantee the above considerations, but also to prevent the state from collapsing into anarchy.

Like Turkey, KUWAIT AND SAUDI ARABIA (at least) will want a strong regime to prevent Iraq from turning into another Afghanistan. The Gulf Cooperation Council (GCC) states may also oppose a significant role for Iraq's Shi'a in a new regime. For that reason, and to prevent setting a bad precedent for their own populations, they may fight U.S. efforts to establish a democratic government in Baghdad. On the other hand, the Kuwaitis (and possibly the Saudis, depending on the circumstances) might see a lengthy U.S. occupation as useful to their own security.

IRAN may hope to see the Shi'a dominate a new Iraqi regime. They may also oppose a new Iraqi regime with heavy ties to the United States. In particular, Tehran may well want to see an end to the U.S. military presence in Iraq and so may intrigue to bring to power a regime that will quickly show the American troops the door. In a worst case scenario, an Iranian regime dominated by the worst hardline extremists might incite Shi'i insurgents to go after American targets in the hope of convincing the United States to quit Iraq prematurely.

For its part, JORDAN will angle for a new regime that will continue to provide it with inexpensive oil. In addition, it may seek a weak Iraq, to minimize its own security concerns. At the extreme, it is even possible that Amman might entertain the possibility of restoring the Hashemite monarchy to Iraq.

Conquering and Occupying Iraq

SYRIA AND EGYPT will probably want a weak regime in Baghdad, no matter what its orientation or composition. For Egypt, Iraq is a potential competitor for leadership of the Arab world. For Syria, it is a large and potentially powerful neighbor. Syria too will likely be uncomfortable with a large U.S. military presence in Iraq for a protracted period. Despite protestations to the contrary, Cairo and Damascus might not be averse to the collapse of the Iraqi state.

OTHER ARAB STATES will doubtless seek to end the American occupation as soon as possible and, in the name of countering neocolonialism, may support a new regime independent of U.S. influence.

It will be a major task for the United States to chart a course among these conflicting interests while also accommodating both U.S. strategic interests and popular demands. The major U.S. interests in the region are the free flow of inexpensive oil and the prevention of a hostile regional state becoming so strong as to be able to threaten this or other U.S. interests (such as the security of American allies, including Israel, Jordan, and Egypt). These interests would argue for either a strong Iraq under heavy American influence or a more independent but weaker Iraq. Some of Iraq's neighbors (and America's allies) will object to either or both of these alternatives. On the other hand, Americans may demand some sort of democracy in Iraq: Their troops will have died conquering the country and it will be highly unpalatable to the U.S. electorate for those soldiers and pilots to have died simply to replace one dictator with another. This too could create real consternation among regional states, which might openly oppose or covertly work to bring down a democratic government.

Who Pays?

An additional consideration for the occupation phase of an

invasion will be financing the presence of U.S. military forces in the country. Maintaining tens of thousands of U.S. military personnel in Iraq for a period of two to five years will not be cheap. One obvious solution would be to use revenue from Iraqi oil exports to finance the American occupation. Yet, Iraqis may object: Iraq's oil exports are likely to be quite limited in the aftermath of an invasion, and most Iraqis will want to use any income to rebuild their country. In this case, it may be necessary for the United States to establish a burden-sharing agreement to finance the long-term presence of U.S. military personnel during the occupation period by taking a percentage of Iraqi oil export revenues but relying more heavily on contributions from Iraq's neighbors (which will benefit most from Saddam's fall) and Western allies, like Japan and Germany, which may want to support the operation but will not want to send troops.

END STATE

The ultimate end state is an Iraq with an effective government that does not threaten regional stability. This option offers some assurance that this end state will be achieved, but not without extraordinary diplomatic and military efforts. The military campaign itself would require almost half of the U.S. military's available might, as well as an international and regional coalition. No matter how extreme the provocation that caused the United States to act, the decision to invade a sovereign state and depose its ruler would add many new twists and layers of complexity to the fragile and volatile geopolitics of the Persian Gulf region. Nonetheless, invasion and occupation is an option in which the United States controls its own and Iraq's destiny. Moreover, a powerful case can be made that such an effort would rid Iraq, the region, and the world of a dangerous ruler who has caused much unnecessary suffering. For that reason alone, it deserves to be considered.

Conquering and Occupying Iraq

ADVANTAGES

Invading and occupying Iraq would have several benefits for the region, the world, and the United States. This policy option would achieve the following goals:

- *Be conclusive and decisive.* Saddam Husayn and his regime would not only be eliminated, but the United States would ensure that a nonthreatening Iraqi government is firmly ensconced before leaving the area. Washington will not have to deal with the problem of Saddam after an invasion. By removing the constant need to devote American resources, diplomacy, and attention to containment, the United States will have greater resources to devote to other international issues.

- *Make the defeat of Saddam's forces eminently achievable.* Whereas an invasion would incur significant costs and involve many unexpected turns of events, the end is almost assured. The Iraqi military would require a miracle to defeat the U.S. armed forces if the U.S. military were allowed to prosecute operations with all necessary force. This is a labor-intensive, but by no means impossible, set of goals.

- *Initial success would be determined by the U.S.-led coalition, not by Saddam.* To the extent that it manages coalition relations well, the United States will control its own destiny in the region rather than constantly responding to Saddam Husayn's actions. Invasion allows Washington to move the confrontation with Baghdad into the arena in which the United States has the greatest advantage over Iraq: conventional military operations.

- *Remove a major source of instability in a vital region or the world.* Saddam himself is the greatest single obstacle to stability in the Gulf region. His ouster would result in a more peaceful region and would eliminate the threat from Iraq to the free flow of Gulf oil. With Saddam gone, the region could concentrate more on economic development. In particular, Saudi Arabia could shift spending from arms purchases to desperately needed reforms of its financial, educational, and social welfare systems. Oil prices might even decline once the threat of disruption by Iraq had been removed.

- *Free Iraq from the rule of Saddam Husayn and the crippling economic sanctions imposed by the international community.* An invasion would meet the humanitarian interests of ending one of the most horrific dictatorships of the twentieth century. The long suffering of the Iraqi people under Saddam's rule and the sanctions regime will end.

- *Transform Iraq into an important economic partner in the region, open to U.S. businesses.* Iraq's oil reserves are at least the second largest in the world; they may well be the largest. U.S. oil companies could reap considerable profits if the Iraqi oil market were reopened after an invasion. Prior to the Gulf War, Iraq was a considerable importer of Western agricultural and manufactured products. In particular, after an invasion, any successor regime is likely to privilege American economic interests in Iraq as a means of currying favor with Washington. (By contrast, if sanctions were lifted with Saddam still in power, he almost certainly would exclude American companies and try to reward those countries that had helped him escape the embargo.)

- *Uncover and destroy Iraq's WMD capability.* The removal of these weapons will greatly contribute to the peace and stability of the region.

- *Punish a rogue dictator, thus sending an important signal to others.* Iran, Libya, North Korea, and other states would likely moderate their worst behavior were they to see solidarity, determination, and resolve of the international community in this matter. An invasion would be a powerful reinforcement of the message the United States has already sent with its air strikes against Libya in 1986, naval and air battles with Iran in 1988, and Operation Desert Storm in 1991—that aggression and terrorism will not be tolerated.

- *Remove a major source of friction with U.S. allies—both in the region and in the UN Security Council.* The great powers will no longer be rent by differences over how to deal with Saddam Husayn and Iraq.

Liabilities and Risks

Despite the above advantages, pursuing a policy of invasion and occupation could lead to the following difficulties for U.S. policymakers and the military:

- *Saddam might lash out with WMD.* In the past, Saddam has been deterred from employing weapons of mass destruction against opponents who could respond in kind (Israel and the United States in particular), for fear of provoking a massive response. With his survival clearly threatened by the invasion, Saddam would have little incentive to refrain from employing every weapon in his arsenal. This could cause a great number of deaths and force the United States (or Israel, if that were the target of his attacks) to retaliate in ways that it otherwise would prefer not to do.

- *The aftermath of an invasion could be far more difficult than the fighting itself.* The United States could find it extremely difficult to rebuild Iraq and establish a new government there. Iraq may not be ready for true democracy, or regional allies may oppose the precedent of Washington imposing democracy on a Middle Eastern state by force—or both may be the case. Most Iraqi elites inside the country have been tainted by Saddam's regime, and the opposition outside the country has both little support and a questionable ability to govern Iraq judiciously. Iraq's neighbors will almost certainly attempt to manipulate events inside the country to produce a new regime favorable to themselves.

- *An end game in Iraq might prove elusive.* The United States could become bogged down in the administration of Iraq. Both the international transitional authority and the new Iraqi government could be less successful and more problematic than anticipated, causing the U.S. military (as in Somalia and Bosnia) to fill the void by taking more and more responsibility for nation-building in Iraq.

- *An invasion may not play well on the "Arab street."* A backlash against a heavy-handed U.S. invasion that caused many Iraqi casualties could cause moderate Arab governments (such as Egypt and Jordan) considerable problems in handling radical elements and their populations in general. An invasion could also conjure images of neocolonialism. In particular, the presence of large numbers of Western military forces in Saudi Arabia—specifically, forces there to invade another Arab state—could prompt terrorism against the United States, its allies, U.S. forces, or the Saudi government.

- *Saddam could flee or stay hidden, as Manuel Noriega did.* Saddam will not "go gently into that dark night." If he were to elude U.S. forces, tracking him down could require a lengthy, politically embarassing manhunt. Worse still, conceivably, he could flee and organize a resistance from outside the country. Merely surviving would make him a hero to many in the Muslim world.

- *The United States might sustain heavy casualties under some scenarios.* The use of WMD, taking of hostages, a house-to-house defense of Baghdad, or other unanticipated problems in the military campaign could result in much greater coalition casualties or could cause the operation to drag on. These "wild card" factors could double, triple, or even quadruple the numbers of expected American and Iraqi casualties. Heavy losses, effective Iraqi strikes during the force buildup phase, or severe collateral damage could undermine the morale of the coalition partners.

• *The United States could be further tarred as an international "bully," prompting other great powers to band together to oppose American unilateralism.* If an invasion took place without UN Security Council approval, the United States could see its international influence lessen as China, Russia, France, and other states form a bloc to oppose similar unilateral decisions.

• *The operation would be expensive.* The Gulf War cost roughly $55 billion, most of which was defrayed by Kuwait, Saudi Arabia, and Japan. An invasion would be at least as expensive, and Kuwait and Saudi Arabia are no longer in a position to absorb such a large percentage of the costs. In addition, the occupation would have to be funded internationally to overcome the considerable expenses not offset by Iraqi oil sales.

• *The campaign would, for a significant period of time, limit U.S. military forces available elsewhere.* Given the decline in U.S. force levels, the units needed for the invasion and occupation of Iraq would greatly reduce America's ability to meet military commitments elsewhere in the world. The Bosnia force would have to be greatly drawn down and there would be little with which to respond to events in Korea or elsewhere, save national guard units not already mobilized for the Gulf campaign.

• *The Gulf states will have less need for weapons, with the result that U.S. arms manufacturers could suffer.*

CONCLUSIONS

Invading and occupying Iraq is the only policy option the United States could adopt that would ensure Saddam's ouster and the establishment of a new, more pluralistic government in Iraq. Although even an invasion could not guarantee that Iraq would never again threaten the vital Gulf region, it clearly offers the best prospects for such an outcome. In addition, an invasion has the virtue of being decisive: It could not be done overnight, but would promise a reasonably speedy end to the confrontation with Iraq, without the protracted agony of the other potential options.

Nevertheless, an invasion would entail significant costs and run some very serious risks. An invasion would not be easy or inexpensive for the United States, either militarily or politically. Whereas the military objectives are eminently achievable, if things were to go wrong, the United States could suffer several thousand casualties. Of far greater consequence, invading Iraq would likely unleash a political maelstrom. The American people could probably be convinced to take this course of action, but European, East Asian, and Middle Eastern populations may require far more convincing. Moreover, before the United States can contemplate invading Iraq it will have to find a solution to the riddle of how to handle Iraq's neighbors and their competing interests in an Iraqi successor regime. If invasion is the course the United States chooses to take, doing it right will require a lot of thought, much diplomatic ground work, and comprehensive planning long before the first tanks are loaded onto ships bound for Saudi Arabia.

AN ALTERNATIVE FRAMEWORK
Support Iraqi Liberation

Patrick L. Clawson

Supporting Iraqi "liberation" holds that with modest levels of U.S. political, financial, and military support, the main Iraqi opposition organization—the Iraq National Congress (INC)—could liberate the Iraqi people, ultimately leading to the installation of a democratic, pro-Western government in Baghdad. This approach assumes that there is a well-organized national opposition coalition already operating, that Saddam's army is weak relative to the opposition, and that an armed opposition force could readily defeat the regime. By contrast, the analysis in the earlier chapters more or less shares a common analytical framework that says the Iraqi opposition is weak, Saddam Husayn is relatively strong, and a large-scale military campaign would be needed to defeat his forces.

If the analytical framework assumed in this chapter is valid, replacing Saddam with a democratic, pro-Western government becomes a potentially low-cost, high-gain option. If the paradigm used in the other chapters is valid, achieving Saddam's overthrow would be difficult. Thus, in deciding what policy to adopt towards Iraq, the first question to ask is, Which analytical framework is correct?

Because what distinguishes this chapter from the earlier chapters is the analytical framework it uses, that paradigm is discussed here at length. The policies implied by

---

With profound thanks for the detailed assistance of Max Singer, who dissents from the analysis presented here.

---

the framework are described in less detail, in part because there is overlap between the policies proposed in this chapter and those in the earlier chapter on undermining or overthrowing Saddam. The difference is that "liberate" suggests that "undermine" and "overthrow" pose a false dilemma in assuming a contradiction between providing the opposition with modest military support and achieving the maximum goal of a pro-Western Iraq with a pluralistic government. Instead, "liberate" posits that conditions in Iraq would allow maximum goals to be attained with limited means.

GOALS

"Liberate" calls for the United States to provide the INC with the limited means it believes it would need to overthrow the Ba'th regime. This policy does not imply that the United States has to ensure that it would succeed, although the policy is predicated on the assumption that conditions in Iraq are such that success is likely. For the U.S. government, the goal of the "liberate" policy is the removal of the current regime and its replacement with a more representative, pro-Western government rooted in Iraqi society—one that would threaten neither its neighbors nor the security of the region.

It is neither practical nor legitimate for the United States, as a matter of course, to remove governments when it disapproves of their policies or believes that they govern badly or cruelly. Therefore, any U.S. interference in the internal affairs of other countries must at least demonstrate that the danger posed by the government to U.S. interests must be severe. Saddam represents a grave threat to U.S. interests. Moreover, according to the proponents of liberate, because a well-organized opposition committed to a military option already exists, U.S. intervention in Iraqi affairs would be minimal.

DESCRIPTION OF THE FRAMEWORK AND POLICY

The Political Strength of the Opposition

In 1992, leaders and representatives from essentially all of the communities in Iraq created the INC as a national movement to overthrow and replace the Ba'th regime. They also agreed, in the INC charter, on the broad procedures for constituting a democratic government once the Ba'th regime was toppled. Moreover, all elements, including Kurds and Shi'is, agreed that Iraqi national integrity and the current borders would be preserved after the Ba'th regime was replaced.

The INC operated in the North of Iraq until Saddam's forces invaded Irbil, within the U.S.-established safe haven, in August 1996. During that time, the INC under the leadership of its elected head, Ahmad Chalabi, established and operated newspapers, radio stations, and other organizations, and established a lightly armed military force. Since August 1996, the INC headquarters has been outside Iraq.

The United States was closely involved in the creation of the INC, one of whose original components was a group of former Ba'thists and army officers organized and controlled by the United States. Through the Central Intelligence Agency (CIA), Washington provided most of the INC's funding until 1996.

The INC has had its problems over the years, but at times it has more accurately forecast events inside Iraq than have Western intelligence sources. The INC believes that it has strong support in Iraq. Chalabi and the INC have become widely known in Iraq, in part owing to frequent attacks on them in the controlled Iraqi press, especially since their defeat at the hands of Iraqi forces in 1996. Saddam's propaganda machine focuses on past CIA support for the INC. The extensive attacks could suggest that Saddam is concerned about the continued political importance of the INC in Iraq.

Support Iraqi Liberation

The Centrality of U.S. Support

An important element in Iraqi popular support for the INC, or any other opposition group, is the degree to which it is seen as having the full support of the United States. Thus, if the United States were to reject the INC and throw its weight behind some other group trying to overthrow the Ba'th, most Iraqis would support that group, despite their commitment to the INC. Whereas most Iraqis would like to see Saddam replaced, they are afraid to support any opposition unless they think it is likely to succeed in removing Saddam. Similarly, a number of governments in the region would like to see Saddam replaced but will not support the Iraqi opposition unless they are convinced that it will succeed.

In Iraq and throughout the region, people believe that the United States is the single most important factor in determining whether Saddam and the Ba'th can be overthrown. U.S. support is perceived to be the *sine qua non* for any group hoping to overthrow the Ba'th, owing to the implicit assumption that if the United States wants an opposition group to succeed, it will succeed. Conversely, U.S. inaction has the effect of undercutting opposition efforts and preserving Ba'th power. Predictions that the opposition is doomed to failure thus become self-fulfilling prophecies. Therefore, U.S. support is a crucial variable determining the fate of the opposition.

It is not clear, however, what level of U.S. commitment is required to convince Iraqis and others that supporting anti-Saddam efforts does not pose an unacceptable risk. Many may insist on a high degree of U.S. commitment because they perceive a pattern of past U.S. indecision about replacing Saddam. U.S. forces ended the 1991 Gulf War precipitately, leaving Saddam with the Republican Guard divisions he needed to remain in power. Then the United States provided no support during the 1991 popular uprising that shook Saddam's control of fourteen of Iraq's eighteen provinces. Since 1991, U.S. support for opposition forces, be they the INC or coup-plotting Ba'thists, has been inconsistent and often inept.

If Washington were to make a major committment to the INC, it should provide the type of material aid entailed in "undermine" as well as highly visible political support. The U.S. government should organize public meetings between INC leaders and senior members of the U.S. administration and should encourage other governments to do the same. Consideration should be given to recognizing the INC as the provisional government of Iraq, at least after it has established a strong foothold inside the country. International organizations could be encouraged to recognize this provisional government as the legitimate voice of Iraq. The United States should make it clear privately that it favors financial support by others for the INC or a successor opposition group. Individual Americans should be allowed, and even encouraged, to provide training and other assistance to the INC or its successor.

In public statements by officials at various levels, the United States would say it would be pleased if a popular democratic opposition movement were to replace a regime that rules on the basis of repression and that threatens aggression and the use of weapons of mass destruction (WMDs). Washington would not, however, overtly advocate the replacement of the Iraqi government, because this is a decision that only the Iraqi people can make and because such a stance would bring into question the authenticity and legitimacy of the INC and the government it hopes to establish.

The Strength of the Iraqi Army

This alternative analytical framework contends that Saddam's forces are so weak that even a small, lightly-armed opposition force could cause their collapse or defeat them in battle. Many divisions are at less than half strength and have not conducted serious field training since 1991. Tanks and other vehicles in these divisions are poorly maintained. Morale has been undermined by low pay and poor living conditions. Even the six divisions of Republican Guard—which, compared to the regular army, are better cared for and more loyal—are no longer as formidable as they were seven years ago, and they are also below authorized strength. An important problem Saddam's troops would face is their lack of mobility, which could hinder them from mounting an effective defense of the regime.

To be sure, Saddam's army—despite all its problems—could put down a popular uprising by unarmed or lightly armed civilians, especially if it were to use attack helicopters and combat aircraft, as long as the soldiers did not care about how many civilians they killed. Accordingly, to overthrow the Ba'th regime, the Iraqi people need a military force to protect them and eventually to bring about the collapse or defeat of Saddam's army.

A MILITARY STRATEGY FOR THE INC

The INC believes it could raise an infantry force of about 10,000 men, consisting largely of former soldiers and officers from the Iraqi army, within about a year. (The INC itself created a considerably more modest force in 1994, when it was receiving less assistance from the United States than assumed here.) Such a force would be equipped with light weapons, such as machine guns, mortars, and man-portable anti-tank and anti-aircraft weapons, and it would rely on off-road trucks and other nonarmored vehicles for transport and mobility. If that force were to achieve a number of quick, early victories, it is possible that the Iraqi divisions facing it would surrender or that many of their soldiers would desert. In that case, the INC forces might grow more rapidly than anticipated.

The INC approach to defeating the Ba'th regime would involve initially taking the Kurdish areas in the North, the Shi'i areas in the South, and the unpopulated area in western Iraq and establishing a provisional government on that territory. If this were achieved, the Iraqi government would be cut off from most of its oilfields and would be unable to export oil. Its only access to the outside world might be via Iran. The Ba'th regime would have grave problems surviving if most of Iraq's territory and its primary economic resource—oil—were in the hands of a provisional government led by the INC. Among other things, countries that have supported Saddam because of his control of Iraq's huge oil deposits could be tempted to switch sides, or at least to provide fewer diplomatic favors to Saddam. With his flow of money largely cut off, Saddam could lose much of his influence and his ability to threaten. Moreover, the INC provisional government could have enough money (from the oil it controls) and manpower (from former soldiers and the population of the area the INC controls) to organize a fairly significant army.

All in all, "liberate" argues that there are reasons to believe that the INC could gradually liberate the country and eventually achieve a military victory over the regime of Saddam Husayn. Although this is a gamble, success would be a major triumph for U.S. interests.

Limited U.S. Military Support

It is widely believed that protecting Iraqi civilians in areas liberated by the opposition would be a demanding task requiring a very large force. This could be true if Baghdad had a free hand to use its airpower. No opposition group could build a force strong enough to withstand the combined weight of Saddam's ground and air forces. But America can, with little effort and risk, constrain Saddam's airforce. U.S. aircraft would be called on to shoot down any Iraqi plane used to attack opposition forces, and the United States would ensure that Iraqi aircraft could not deliver a significant number of strikes against the opposition. It would then be up to the opposition to handle Saddam's ground forces.

For the training of the opposition forces, the INC proposes to rely mainly on Arab trainers, including defectors from Saddam's army. U.S. forces might also be involved in the training of INC forces, as well as in the evaluation of their training, plans, equipment, and logistical preparations. Experience elsewhere, however, has shown that such training could be accomplished with the involvement of only a few hundred Americans.

The United States would probably have to finance arms for the opposition, but the cost could be kept limited by using funds from blocked Iraqi assets or by providing the arms on credit, against future oil deliveries.

ADVANTAGES

In policy terms, "liberate" would have the following advantages:

- *It presents the possibility of a near-ideal outcome.* An INC victory would mean the creation of a democratic, pro-Western government in a key Arab country, the tranformation of Iraq into a force for stability in the region, and the end to the Iraqi WMD threat. A victory by the INC might well be one of the most promising developments in the Middle East in fifty years.
- *It involves no anticipated use of U.S. ground forces and limited use of air forces.* If things go according to plan, the INC victory would be achieved without the commitment of U.S. ground forces and the significant casualties this could entail.
- *It could generate some international support.* Strong U.S. leadership and commitment for a definitive solution to the Saddam problem will lead some governments to rally to the U.S. side, out of principle or because they want to be in the winning camp.

LIABILITIES AND RISKS

Among the policy's disadvantages are the following:

- *Potential for a crisis.* Public U.S. support for the opposition could spark a protracted crisis once the policy is adopted. Saddam could resume blatant obstruction of UN weapons inspections or expel the UN Special Commission on Iraq (UNSCOM) altogether; support for sanctions might wane further; and Saddam might initiate a desperate military gambit to scuttle efforts to establish the INC, drawing the United States into a major military confronation.

- *Defeat resulting in bloodbath.* If the key assumptions undergirding "liberate" prove to be unfounded (if the INC proves ineffective in combat; if the INC is unable to hold onto liberated areas with a small, lightly armed force; if Saddam's forces demonstrate a modicum of skill and tenacity; or if the INC's tactics prove inadequate), the INC might find itself in a debacle that would seriously hurt U.S. interests in the region. In these circumstances, the United States could have to choose between acquiescing in a massacre of INC forces or deepening its military involvement, which could include the dispatch of ground forces to southern and northern Iraq to prevent the annihilation of the opposition.

- *No quick-fix.* Supporting the opposition does not guarantee a quick solution to the problem of Iraq. Even if the opposition progresses rapidly to the point at which it could seize and hold portions of Iraq, Saddam might hang on in Baghdad and its surroundings for some time. It could be years before the opposition finally emerges victorious.

- *Public statements may not be convincing.* Central to "liberate" is a belief that U.S. public support would provide a dramatic boost to the opposition. Yet, given the checkered U.S. record of supporting opposition to Saddam, public statements may not give Iraqis and those in neighboring countries enough confidence to take the necessary risks. It is unclear whether even a strongly stated commitment could overcome skepticism toward the United States based on years of experience, including what are seen as multiple betrayals.

- *Possible use of chemical or biological weapons.* Although Saddam might be deterred from using chemical or biological weapons against either INC or U.S. forces, it is prudent to assume that deterrence could fail if the INC is successful and he feels he has nothing to lose.

CONCLUSIONS

This analytical framework argues that a well-organized and potentially effective national opposition coalition already exists, that Saddam's army is weak relative to the opposition, and that a lightly armed, highly motivated, and highly mobile armed opposition force could readily defeat the regime. If this is correct, a decision to back the opposition in a bid to topple the regime offers hope for a democratic, pro-Western Iraq, at relatively little cost and risk. Success would be a major triumph for the United States. Yet, such a policy is based on a series of contested assumptions and thus is a high-stakes gamble. It is a risky strategy that could lead to the slaughter of opposition forces, a humiliating defeat for the United States, and a grave setback to U.S. interests in the region.

APPENDIX
Background Information on Iraq

Glossary of Terms

IRAQ NATIONAL CONGRESS (INC). Created in 1992 to coordinate the activities of the various Iraqi opposition groups against Saddam Husayn's regime. This umbrella organization is headed by Ahmad Chalabi and based primarily in London. From 1992 to 1996 the INC maintained a presence in northern Iraq, where it sought to build a force of dedicated fighters and establish a network of informants, recruiters, and agitators throughout the country. The regime's attack on Irbil, where the INC had its center of activity, smashed the nascent INC infrastructure in northern Iraq. Some 100 INC personnel were arrested and shot by Saddam's secret police, and nearly 900 others were airlifted by the United States to safety on Guam.

KURDISH DEMOCRATIC PARTY (KDP). One of the two main Kurdish militias. The KDP is the oldest and most storied of the Iraqi Kurdish resistance groups, having been founded by Mullah Mustafah Barzani in 1946. Today, the KDP is led by Mulla Mustafah's son, Masoud Barzani, and controls most of northern and western Kurdistan. In 1996, the KDP threw in its lot with Saddam's regime and colluded in the Iraqi attack on Irbil.

"MATERIAL BREACH." In August 1991, the United Nations Security Council passed Resolution 707 which declared Iraq in "material breach of the relevant provisions of Resolution 687," which set out the terms of the 1991 ceasefire. Since then, the term has come to signify the strongest condemnation of Iraqi violations by the Security Council. Further Security Council resolutions and presidential statements reaffirming Iraq's material breach of Resolution 687 led eventually to American, British, and French cruise missile and air strikes against Iraq in January 1993. This established a precedent that any declaration that Iraq was in "material breach" of a resolution constituted the Security Council's permission to any member state (although in practice, the United States and Great Britain) to use force against Iraq to compel Baghdad to comply with that resolution. The Security Council has not found Iraq in material breach since June 1993.

MULTILATERAL INTERCEPTION FORCE (MIF). A task force of warships from various coalition nations that enforces the embargo on Iraq by monitoring naval traffic to and from Iraqi ports. The MIF regularly intercepts and inspects suspect vessels in the Persian Gulf to ensure that contraband is not smuggled into Iraq.

NO-DRIVE ZONE. In October 1994, Baghdad began deploying armored divisions of the Republican Guard to the Kuwaiti border, possibly to attack Kuwait. The Security Council responded by passing Resolution 949, which demanded that Iraq withdraw its forces south of the thirty-second parallel and return to their "original positions" immediately. Based on this resolution, the United States declared a "no-drive zone" coterminous with the southern no-fly zone. Baghdad was warned that if it attempted to move additional ground forces south of the thirty-second parallel in excess of the handful of divisions that had been present on October 7, 1994, the United States would respond with all necessary means.

NO-FLY ZONES. There are two no-fly zones over Iraq. Operation Northern Watch oversees the northern no-fly zone, which covers all Iraqi territory north of the thirty-sixth parallel (running just below Irbil). American and British combat aircraft participate in Northern Watch, flying from the Turkish airbase at Incirlik. Operation Southern Watch oversees the southern no-fly zone. Initially, that covered all Iraqi territory south of the thirty-second parallel. The United States, Britain, and France did not ask for formal Security Council approval for the establishment of the no-fly zones but instead cited the terms of Resolution 678, which authorizes all member states to use "all necessary means" to see that Iraq complies with other Security Council resolutions. In response to Saddam's forces reoccupying parts of Iraqi Kurdistan in 1996, the United States and Britain extended the southern no-fly zone to the thirty-third parallel (running just below Baghdad). Iraqi aircraft, including helicopters, are forbidden to fly in either of the no-fly zones. As a result of these zones, roughly 60 percent of Iraqi airspace is off limits to Iraqi aircraft.

PATRIOTIC UNION OF KURDISTAN (PUK). One of the two main Kurdish militias, the PUK was founded in June 1975 by Jalal Talabani in opposition to Mullah Mustafah Barzani, then the leader of the KDP. Talabani and his followers broke away from the KDP after the disastrous defeat of the Kurds in March 1975, when Saddam's deal with the Shah of Iran (the Algiers Accord) led Iran to abandon the Kurds to the Iraqi army. Today, the PUK is still led by Talabani and controls most of southern and eastern Iraqi Kurdistan. In 1996, Talabani formed an alliance of sorts with the Iranians that allowed him to score several impressive victories against the rival KDP. These PUK successes were apparently the spark that led the KDP to strike its deal with the regime in Baghdad.

PKK (KURDISTAN WORKERS' PARTY). The Kurdistan Workers' Party (*Partiya Karkari Kurdistan,* in Turkish) is the principal Kurdish group fighting for Kurdish secession from Turkey. It was founded in the mid-1970s but first came to prominence in 1984 with a series of attacks on Turkish elements in southeastern Turkey that left 12,000 people dead by 1994. The PKK employs both insurgent operations and outright terrorism in its operations. Although its leader, Abdallah Ocalan, is in Syria, most PKK fighters are based in Iraq and carry out their operations against Turkey from there. These activities have led to repeated Turkish incursions into northern Iraq to try to smash the PKK base infrastructure there.

REPUBLICAN GUARD FORCES COMMAND (RGFC). The Republican Guard originally served as the garrison of the city of Baghdad and the praetorian guards for the regime itself. Its purpose was to defend the regime against an army coup or popular revolt. During the Iran–Iraq and Gulf Wars, however, Saddam transformed the RGFC into Iraq's elite conventional military force. He expanded the Guard from just a handful of brigades in 1980 to six divisions by 1988, and to twelve by 1991. The best soldiers and officers in the army were recruited into the Guard, and they were provided the best equipment, training, and support Baghdad had to offer. As a result, the Republican Guard was able to achieve a higher degree of competence than the regular army. The RGFC was largely responsible for Iraq's dramatic victories over Iran in 1988 and its rapid conquest of Kuwait in 1990. Against the U.S.-led coalition during the Gulf War, essentially only the Republican Guard stood and fought against superior American and British units. The Guard fought extremely hard but was completely outmatched in skill, technology, and numbers by the coalition armies. Today, the RGFC again consists of six divisions—three armored, one mechanized infantry, and two infantry—along with several independent special forces brigades, and it is used to defend Baghdad and bolster the regular army in its battles with Kurdish and Shi'i insurgents.

Although the Guard gave over some of its regime-protection functions to the Special Republican Guard (see below), it still serves as the primary bulwark of the regime either against an army coup or a popular revolt. Indeed, it was primarily Guard divisions that put down the series of revolts that shook Iraq after the conclusion of the Gulf War. Because it still plays this role, Saddam goes to some pains to ensure its loyalty. Many

Guard personnel (particularly officers) come from Saddam's hometown of Tikrit, are members of his al-Bu Nasir tribe, or belong to the Jubbur, Dulaym, 'Ubayd, or Shammar tribal confederations, which are strong supporters of the regime. The Guard does not report along the normal military chain of command but instead has its own chain of command that leads eventually to Saddam's second son, Qusayy, who is also in charge of his father's internal security apparatus. Guard personnel receive special perquisites, better pay, and larger rations than the rest of the population.

SANCTIONS. In response to the Iraqi invasion of Kuwait, the UN Security Council levied a wide range of sanctions against Iraq. On August 6, 1990, it passed UN Security Council Resolution 661, which banned the import of Iraqi products and the export to Iraq of any goods other than food, medicine, and other strictly humanitarian supplies. Resolution 661 also froze all overseas Iraqi assets. Two months later, Resolution 670 expanded the sanctions to impose a total flight ban on Iraq (no planes could fly to or from the country). Following Operation Desert Storm, the Security Council passed Resolution 686, which demanded that Iraq accept liability for all damage arising from the war and that it release all Kuwaitis arrested by Iraqi forces during the occupation. Resolution 687 created a compensation fund for the victims of Iraqi aggression, to be funded from Iraqi oil exports. In 1996, Iraq accepted Resolution 986, which allowed Iraq to sell a limited amount of oil ($4.1 billion per year, later increased by Resolution 1153 to $10.7 billion) to pay for the import of food and medicine under close UN supervision.

SPECIAL REPUBLICAN GUARD (SRG). When Baghdad expanded the Republican Guard to turn it into a conventional military force, it created the Special Republican Guard to fill the role previously played by the Republican Guard. The SRG consists of three to five brigades and 20,000 to 30,000 personnel.

It provides the garrison for the city of Baghdad, protects regime facilities, guards regime leadership, and has also been entrusted with the mission of guarding Iraq's clandestine weapons of mass destruction programs. The SRG is well-equipped by Iraqi standards. It is drawn overwhelmingly from Tikritis, members of Saddam's al-Bu Nasir tribe, and others with a close personal tie to Saddam. Like the RGFC, the SRG reports directly to Qusayy Saddam Husayn.

UNITED NATIONS SECURITY COUNCIL. The UN Security Council constitutes the highest deliberative organ within the UN constellation. It is responsible for UN decisions on issues of war, peace, and diplomacy. The Security Council consists of fifteen members, who rotate as president of the council every two months, with the president having responsibility for setting the agenda and moderating procedure. Five countries (the United States, United Kingdom, Russia, China, and France) are permanent members of the council and possess a veto power over any or all Security Council actions. The other ten countries change every two years. Although these eight are drawn from the General Assembly, most of these seats traditionally go to representatives from certain groups of countries: There is always an Arab country represented, a European country, an Asian country, a South American country, an African country, and so forth.

The Security Council has been the primary agent for handling the problem of Iraq since its invasion of Kuwait in 1990. It demanded that Iraq withdraw from Kuwait, authorized the use of force to evict Iraqi forces from Kuwait, and mandated the restrictions on Iraq following the success of Operation Desert Storm. The Security Council also is responsible for the maintenance of the sanctions and inspections regimes on Iraq: Every six months, in April and October, UNSCOM must submit a report to the Security Council regarding Iraq's compliance with Resolution 687. Every 90 days, the Security Council receives a sanctions committee report concerning implementation of the various embargoes on Iraq, every 60 days it meets to consider lifting the economic sanctions on Iraq, and every 120 days it meets to consider lifting the embargo on arms sales to Iraq. To date, no member of the Security Council has even proposed a new resolution requesting that sanctions be lifted or modified, because Iraq has consistently failed to comply in full with its various Security Council obligations. Yet, if Iraq is to have the sanctions lifted or modified, it will require a two-thirds majority vote in the Security Council, without a veto by any of the permanent five members. In other words, as long as the Security Council does not vote to lift the sanctions, they remain in full effect.

UNITED NATIONS SPECIAL COMMISSION ON IRAQ (UNSCOM). UNSCOM was created in 1991 to implement the articles of Resolution 687, which forbids Iraq from possessing weapons of mass destruction and ballistic missiles with ranges in excess of 150 kilometers. UNSCOM consists of scientists, technicians, diplomats, linguists, and military experts from a wide range of nations. They are responsible for verifying whether Iraq has met its disarmament obligations. Specifically, UNSCOM (in conjunction with the International Atomic Energy Agency, which is responsible for Iraq's nuclear program) must determine whether Iraq has dismantled all of its proscribed weapons and the facilities for manufacturing such weapons. UNSCOM has authority to inspect anywhere in Iraq to ascertain whether Iraq has met these obligations. In addition, UNSCOM is responsible for monitoring Iraq indefinitely to ensure that Baghdad does not try to rebuild its arsenal. UNSCOM has already put in place many elements of the long-term monitoring regime, which function at several suspect sites in Iraq today.

WEAPONS OF MASS DESTRUCTION (WMD). A short-hand term for chemical, biological, and nuclear weapons.

Selected UN Security Council Resolutions

R**esolution 661** levied the original set of sanctions on Iraq on August 6, 1990, in the wake of the Iraqi invasion of Kuwait. Specifically, it calls on all states to prevent the following:

- "the import into their territories of all commodities and products originating in Iraq or Kuwait exported therefrom after the date of the present resolution";
- "any dealings by their nationals or their flag vessels or in their territories in any commodities or products originating in Iraq or Kuwait and exported therefrom"; and
- "the sale or supply by their nationals or from their territories or using their flag vessels of any commodities or products including weapons or any other military equipment, whether or not originating in their territories but not including supplies intended strictly for medical purposes, and, in humanitarian circumstances, foodstuffs. . . ."

The resolution also calls on all states to "not make available to the Government of Iraq, or to any commercial, industrial or public utility undertaking in Iraq or Kuwait, any funds or any other financial or economic resources. . . ."

In addition, Resolution 661 created the so-called "Sanctions Committee" that oversees the implementation of the various regulations on Iraq. The resolution "decides to establish . . . a Committee of the Security Council consisting of all the members of the Council, to undertake the [aforementioned] tasks and to report on its work to the Council . . . ."

Resolution 687 was drafted during the month of negotiations after the successful liberation of Kuwait and adopted on April 3, 1991. This resolution sets out the terms for a formal ceasefire between the coalition and the government of Iraq. As such, it contains many of the key provisions for Iraqi behavior determined by the Security Council. Resolution 687

- demands that "Iraq and Kuwait respect the inviolability of the international boundary," and to this end it calls for a "demilitarized zone, which is hereby established, extending ten kilometers into Iraq and five kilometers into Kuwait";
- "decides that Iraq shall unconditionally accept the destruction, removal, or rendering harmless, under international supervision, of . . . all chemical and biological weapons . . . [and] all ballistic missiles with a range greater than 150 km";
- empowers the secretary general to create a UN special commission (UNSCOM) to see that Iraq complies with the above conditions;
- further demands that Iraq "unconditionally agree not to acquire or develop nuclear weapons," and charges the International Atomic Energy Agency to "place all of [Iraq's] nuclear-weapon usable materials under the exclusive control, for custody and removal, of the Agency";
- creates "a fund to pay compensation for claims" against Iraq arising from its "unlawful invasion and occupation of Kuwait"—Iraq is to contribute to this fund "based on a percentage of the value of its exports of petroleum and petroleum products";
- explicitly *permits* the "sale or supply to Iraq" of "medicine and health supplies . . . [as well as] foodstuffs"; and
- prohibits the sale to Iraq of any type of weapon or item that could relate to arms.

One important passage of the resolution is paragraph 22, which states, "the prohibitions against the import of commodities and products originating in Iraq and the prohibitions against financial transactions related thereto contained in resolution 661 (1990) shall have no further effect," provided that the Security Council has agreed "that Iraq has completed all actions contemplated in paragraphs 8 to 13." Paragraphs 8-13 concern Iraqi disarmament and the establishment and responsibilities of UNSCOM.

Resolution 688 "condemns the repression of the Iraqi civilian population in many parts of Iraq, including most recently in Kurdish-populated areas." In it, the Security Council demands Iraq "immediately end this repression," "insists that Iraq allow immediate access by international humanitarian organizations to all those in need of assistance in all parts of Iraq," and "appeals to all Member States and to all humanitarian organizations to contribute to these humanitarian relief efforts."

Resolution 986 stems from the Security Council's concern for the "serious nutritional and health situation of the Iraqi population." To provide for "the humanitarian needs of the Iraqi people until the fulfillment by Iraq of the relevant Security Council resolutions, including notably resolution 687 (1991) of 3 April 1991," the Security Council authorizes member states to "permit the import of petroleum and petroleum products originating in Iraq, including financial and other essential transactions directly relating thereto, sufficient to produce a sum not exceeding a total of one billion United States dollars every 90 days." All such imports must be approved by "the Committee established by resolution 661 (1990), in order to ensure the transparency of each transaction." Moreover, payments for these trades must be made directly "by the purchaser . . . into [an] escrow account to be established by the Secretary-General." The resolution allows Turkey to permit the export of Iraqi oil through the Kirkuk–Yumurtalik pipeline, but it stipulates that all funds deposited in the escrow account as a result of sales of Iraqi oil, "shall be used to meet the humanitarian needs of the Iraqi population." In addition, a portion of these funds is to be used "to meet the costs to the United Nations of the independent inspection agents and the certified public accountants and the activities associated with implementation of this resolution." Iraq shall also grant "full freedom of movement and all necessary facilities for the discharge of their duties in the implementation of this resolution."

Resolution 1153 greatly expands the provisions of Resolution 986, nearly tripling the amount of oil Iraq is allowed to export and increasing the range of goods it is allowed to import. Specifically, to deal with the fact that "the population of Iraq continues to face a very serious nutritional and health situation," the Security Council "decides that the authorization given to States by paragraph 1 of resolution 986 (1995) shall permit the import of petroleum and petroleum products . . . sufficient to produce the sum, in the 180-day period . . . not exceeding a total of 5.256 billion United States dollars, of which the amounts recommended by the Secretary-General for the food/nutrition and health sectors should be allocated on a priority basis." Further, it provides for "an interim review of the implementation of this resolution 90 days after the entry in force" of this resolution.

Resolution 1154 includes a Security Council endorsement of "the memorandum of understanding signed by the deputy Prime Minister of Iraq and the Secretary-General on 23 February 1998." This agreement provides for UNSCOM inspection of eight of Saddam Husayn's palaces (the so-called "Presidential Sites) in the company of a group of international diplomats. The resolution requests the "Secretary-General to report to the council as soon as possible with regard to the finalization of procedures for Presidential sites in consultation with the Executive Chairman of the United Nations Special Commission and the Director General of the International Atomic Energy Agency (IAEA)." The resolution also "stresses . . . compliance by the Government of Iraq with its obligations . . . to accord immediate, unconditional, and unrestricted access to the Special Commission and the IAEA," and threatens that "any violation would have severest consequences for Iraq." Finally, the Security Council notes that, "by its failure so far to comply with its relevant obligations, Iraq has delayed the moment when the Council can [lift sanctions as provided by Resolution 687]."

Residual WMD Capabilities

Michael J. Eisenstadt

I raq possesses a substantial residual weapons of mass destruction (WMD) capability, and in any confrontation with
Iraq, Washington will have to deter Baghdad from using
these weapons.[1] If the United States should choose to overthrow Saddam or invade Iraq to forcibly topple Saddam, this
could be particularly difficult. With a hostile army marching
on Baghdad, Saddam is likely to see little reason for restraint
and might lash out with his WMDs in a desperate effort to
stave off his ouster.

CHEMICAL WEAPONS. Iraq is believed to still possess a small
stockpile of lethal agents and munitions that could inflict massive casualties on an unprotected civilian population, though
it probably does not have sufficient quantities of chemical
munitions for effective battlefield use. Iraq is believed to possess precursor chemicals and production equipment that could
enable it to resume production of chemical weapons during a
protracted crisis. Items that remain unaccounted for include

- stocks of blister and nerve agents, possibly including quantities of "VX salt"—a form of the highly lethal nerve agent
that can be stored on a long-term basis;
- more than 600 tons of VX precursors (enough to make
200 tons of the agent) and some 4,000 tons of other precursor chemicals (enough to produce several hundreds of
tons of agent); and
- between 30,000 and 40,000 munitions that could be filled

with chemical *or* biological agents (including some forty-five to seventy al-Husayn missile warheads, 2,000 bombs, 15,000 artillery shells, and 15,000 to 25,000 rockets). The U.S. government believes that if inspections and monitoring were to cease, Iraq could resume production of mustard agent in weeks, sarin within months, and VX in two to three years.

BIOLOGICAL WEAPONS. Iraq probably retains agent seed stocks, growth media, production equipment, and munitions, and it almost certainly has sufficient quantities of biological agent on hand to cause massive casualties among civilians, though it may not yet have perfected the means for effectively disseminating biological warfare agents. Items that remain unaccounted for include

- unknown quantities of seed stock and/or bulk stocks of anthrax, botulinum toxin, clostridium perfringens, afla-toxin, and ricin (Iraq has not produced credible evidence to verify its claim that it unilaterally destroyed all its biological agents and munitions);
- seventeen tons of growth media—enough to grow more than three times the amount of anthrax that Iraq has admitted to thus far;
- equipment that could be used to produce biological agent in dried form, which is a much more effective way to disseminate the agent than the liquid form that Iraq has acknowledged producing;
- possibly more advanced warhead designs than those recovered to date (in the late 1980s Iraq tried to acquire supersonic parachutes that could have been used to build more advanced models); and
- spray equipment that could be used to disseminate agent from manned or unmanned aircraft.

Iraq almost certainly retains a residual biological warfare capability, as some agents (such as anthrax) can be stored and remain viable for decades. Moreover, both the United Nations

Special Commission on Iraq (UNSCOM) and the U.S. government believe that if inspection and monitoring were to cease, Iraq could resume production of biological agents within a matter of days. Some UN inspectors, however, believe that Iraq may currently possess a clandestine biological warfare agent-production capability, which means that the country could be producing biological warfare agents at this time.

BALLISTIC MISSILES. Iraq may retain a small force of operational missiles (locally produced versions of the al-Husayn) equipped with chemical or biological warheads and mounted on mobile launchers. In addition, Iraq has conducted computer-design studies of missiles with proscribed ranges since the 1991 Gulf War, and it has continued efforts to procure components for such missiles—including gyroscopes from scrapped Russian long-range missiles that it obtained in 1995. Because Iraq is permitted to produce missiles with a range of 150km or less, it retains the infrastructure, talent, and know-how needed to reconstitute its missile program rapidly. Thus, were inspections and monitoring to cease, Iraq could produce a missile of proscribed range perhaps within a year, by clustering or stacking missiles currently in its inventory, or by resuming production of the al-Husayn missile.

NUCLEAR WEAPONS. The International Atomic Energy Agency (IAEA) lacks a complete picture of Iraq's prewar nuclear program. Unknowns include the organization of Iraq's nuclear procurement network; the degree of progress toward mastering the production of centrifuge components; the scope of foreign assistance to Iraq's gas centrifuge program; the whereabouts of bomb components produced before the Gulf War (Iraq claims to have destroyed these but has not produced credible evidence); the extent of progress toward creating a viable nuclear weapon (that is, whether Iraq succeeded in manufacturing all the components—other than fissile material—needed for a bomb); and the whereabouts of gram quantities of low-enriched uranium from its calutron program. In addition, thousands of documents that could yield important insights into Iraq's nuclear program remain untranslated. Iraq also possesses a workable bomb design and its cadre of experienced scientists and technicians—who remain together and probably can do paper and computer studies and simulations as well as weapons-design work with little risk of detection. Since the Gulf War, Iraq is suspected of having conducted clandestine theoretical research relating to bottlenecks in its pre-1991 program, which would make it easier to resurrect its program if inspections and monitoring were to cease. The greatest concern here remains the possibility that, were Iraq to acquire fissile material from abroad, it could probably produce an operational nuclear weapon—perhaps within a year—even with inspections and monitoring in place.

NOTE

[1]   The above assessment is based on published U.S., British, and United Nations documents, as well as information disclosed by UN weapons inspectors in the media and various public fora. It highlights how much remains to be done for Iraq to fulfill its obligations to dismantle its WMD capabilities.

Conventional Military Capabilities

Kenneth M. Pollack

I raqi conventional military capabilities remain extremely limited. Iraqi units could offer only token resistance against American or other Western forces, although they could cause significant casualties in certain scenarios. The Iraqi armed forces are capable of defending the state against the militaries of any of their neighbors, with the likely exception of Turkey. Moreover, the Iraqi military would be a formidable adversary for any military campaign waged by the Iraqi opposition. Yet, in the past, the Iraqis have proven incompetent in counterinsurgency operations, and an efficient guerilla force (which the current Iraqi opposition does not even remotely approximate) would likely give Baghdad's armies real difficulty.

NOT EVEN A PAPER TIGER. In 1991, the Iraqi armed forces looked very formidable on paper. At that time, Baghdad boasted as many as 1.4 million men under arms, sixty-six divisions (twelve of them Republican Guard), 5,700 tanks, and more than 700 combat aircraft. Of course, their performance during Operation Desert Storm demonstrated that they were incapable of realizing the potential represented by their numbers. Today, even on paper, the Iraqi armed forces are a pale shadow of even their 1991 form. The Iraqi military currently fields only 400,000 men, twenty-three divisions (six of them Republican Guard), 2,000 tanks, and 200 to 300 combat aircraft.[1] In theory, a force this size could still represent a challenge for the United States, but in actuality, Iraqi

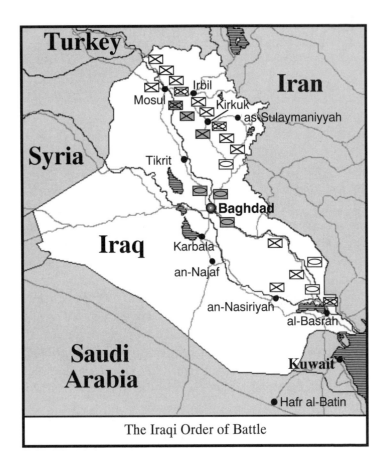

The Iraqi Order of Battle

forces are even less capable today than they were in 1991.

Iraq's equipment holdings leave much to be desired. Most of Iraq's arms are obsolete and it lost most of its advanced weaponry during the Gulf War. For example, Republican Guard divisions that were once equipped entirely with T-72s now must use T-55s. Iraqi forces are also plagued by poor and haphazard maintenance practices, which further reduce their numbers of operable equipment. Iraqi maintenance has never been good—during the Iran–Iraq War, most Iraqi Army formations rarely had more than two-thirds of their vehicles operational at any time. As a result of the UN sanctions, Iraq has been unable to buy spare parts, tools, lubricants, and other supplies, with the result that its maintenance problems have worsened. Many Iraqi weapons have rusted beyond use, lack critical parts, or have been cannibalized to keep other equipment running. To compensate, Baghdad has been forced to demobilize numerous divisions and reduce the numbers of weapons assigned to those remaining.

Iraq's armed forces suffer from other significant shortcomings. During the Gulf War, Iraqi forces were crippled by overcentralized command and control, poor tactical leadership, an inability to take full advantage of their weapons, inadequate attention to reconnaissance, and near total incompetence in battles of maneuver both on the ground and in the air. There is no indication that Iraq has made any progress in remedying these problems. Iraqi training continues to focus on static defensive operations and set-piece offensives. Although Iraqi training invariably features combined arms operations, Iraqi combat formations have demonstrated little ability to implement such operations in other than set-piece maneuvers. Ultimately, Iraqi forces are likely to prove even less flexible and capable than they did during Operation Desert Storm.

IRAQI AIR AND AIR DEFENSE FORCES. Iraq's ground-based air defenses could probably inflict some casualties on U.S. air forces, but they would be overcome quickly by a determined U.S. effort. The Iraqis have been able to reconstruct most of their prewar integrated air defense system. Yet, they have been unable to expand or improve its capabilities, which proved inadequate to the task of defeating U.S. air power in 1991. Indeed, the inability of Iraqi air defenses to deter or defeat periodic raids by the Iranian air force since the war suggests that the Iraqi air defense net remains in worse shape now than it was then. The Iraqis have been practicing some new tricks— such as distancing fire-control radars from surface-to-air missile (SAM) launch units, which makes crews less vulnerable to the high-speed anti-radiation missiles that proved so devastating during the war. But in the past, Iraqi forces have shown an inability to execute the more sophisticated tactics they have occasionally practiced.

Iraqi SAMs are mostly obsolete and lack the capability to shoot down advanced U.S. combat aircraft without a great deal of luck. Many of Iraq's vast array of anti-aircraft guns are inoperable owing to age or poor maintenance, and Baghdad still has not found a solution to the U.S. tactic that proved so successful during the Gulf War: flying above the 10,000-foot ceiling of most Iraqi anti-aircraft guns.

The Iraqi Air Force is unlikely to prove more effective than it was during the Gulf War. Iraqi pilots were exceptionally poor—many could barely fly their planes, let alone dogfight—and were wholly dependent on directions from ground controllers, which were routinely jammed by coalition forces. As a result of the shortages caused by the embargo and the restrictions of the two no-fly zones, Iraqi air force pilots have generally had even fewer flight hours than in the past to practice combat skills. Iraq has not found a solution to the problem of American jamming of its communications, nor has it been able to train its pilots to fight without direction from their ground controllers. Maintenance problems have hit the air force hardest of all, and the war left Iraq with only a handful of advanced fighter aircraft (maybe a dozen operable MiG-29s and possibly twice that number of Mirage F-1 interceptors). If Saddam were to try to contest a new U.S. air campaign, he would probably leave most of the work to his ground-based air defenses for fear of having too many expensive aircraft shot down by American fighters.

CONVENTIONAL RETALIATION. It is unlikely but not inconceivable that if Saddam could not actually stop a U.S. or U.S.-backed military operation, he might go on the offensive with his own conventional forces. Here as well, his options would be quite limited. The destruction of Iraq's logistical assets during the Gulf War—plus its maintenance problems—effectively preclude long-distance armored offensives such as would be needed to threaten key objectives in Saudi Arabia (such as Jubayl or Riyadh) or Jordan (such as Amman or Mafraq). U.S. air interdiction along the limited road networks from Iraq to Saudi Arabia and Jordan would probably make it impossible for Iraq to attack even less important, but closer, objectives such as Hafr al-Batin in Saudi Arabia or Jordan's H-4 air base. In the absence of U.S. forces, Iraq probably could once again overrun Kuwait, but the United States has proven that it can reinforce Kuwait more quickly than Iraq can threaten it. The forces Baghdad currently has in place in southern Iraq lack the combat skills and mobility to be entrusted with such a mission. Consequently, as in 1990 and 1994, Saddam would undoubtedly rely on the Republican Guard for an invasion of Kuwait. In October 1994, the United States demonstrated that in the time it would take for Iraq to move these units to the Kuwaiti border, Washington could deploy far more military power to the region than could Iraq. In addition, the United States currently has more powerful military forces in Kuwait than it did in 1994, and it would therefore need even less time to prepare for battle—and Iraq probably will be reluctant to concentrate the Republican Guard for an offensive, out of fear that it would then be vulnerable to U.S. airstrikes.

Nor does Saddam have much of an airstrike option. First, the Iraqis flew most of their advanced strike aircraft to Iran during the Gulf War. All of Baghdad's Su-24 Fencers are now in Iranian hands, as are most, if not all, of Iraq's Mirage F-1EQ5/6s—the strike variant of the Mirage F-1. Second, Iraq's remaining inventory of attack aircraft consists of older Soviet planes that carry less sophisticated munitions and have shorter ranges, poorer avionics, and less ability to penetrate enemy

Iraq Strategy Review   179

air defenses. These planes realistically could attack targets only in Kuwait, eastern Jordan, northern Saudi Arabia, or south-eastern Turkey, where they would likely face U.S. fighters and Patriot missile batteries that would make short work of any Iraqi attackers.

WORST CASE SCENARIOS. Despite the weakness of the Iraqi armed forces, under certain circumstances they could cause significant casualties to U.S. forces. First, any air effort against Iraq would have to expect to suffer some losses to anti-aircraft guns, surface-to-air missiles, and accidents. In most circum-stances, losses probably would not exceed Desert Storm rates (thirty-eight aircraft lost in 111,000 sorties). Yet, if U.S. air-craft were forced to fight more aggressively than during the Gulf War, these rates could climb significantly. For example, if U.S. air forces were asked to fly larger numbers of close-air support missions and had to fly those missions below 10,000 feet to improve their accuracy, loss rates could increase dra-matically. Such requirements would not be necessary to sup-port a ground invasion of Iraq by U.S. military forces, but they would be essential to support Iraqi opposition forces try-ing either to hold on to captured Iraqi territory (as part of an "undermine" policy) or to march on Baghdad (as part of an "overthrow" policy).

Second, in certain scenarios, Iraqi forces might be able to inflict significant casualties on U.S. ground forces. Without question, the Iraqis could do the most damage if they were willing to fight hard and defend Iraq's cities. Military opera-tions in urban terrain are extremely difficult and greatly di-minish such advantages as superior skill, superior technology, and air support—the precise advantages of the United States over Iraq. If American ground troops were forced to reduce Iraq's cities in house-to-house clearing operations, U.S. forces could suffer thousands of casualties. Yet, given the fragility of Iraqi Army morale, it is difficult to imagine many Iraqi units being willing to fight such battles: Having been defeated in the field, the war would clearly have been lost and most Iraqi troops would be eager to quit the battle. Only the Republican Guard would likely be willing to keep on fighting, as they probably would fear for their well-being after Saddam's fall. Of course, by that point in any invasion scenario, many of the Republican Guard formations would already have been smashed trying to block the American invasion.

NOTE

[1] In the event of a national emergency, such as an invasion of Iraq, Baghdad could probably mobilize another twenty to thirty divisions, but these formations would be equipped with little more than infantry weapons and small numbers of towed artillery; moreover, they would have little time to train. As in the Gulf War, these Iraqi divisions would have very little combat capability and could not handle missions more demanding than static defensive operations against a very weak adversary. Against modern U.S. divisions, these units would likely crumble as they did during Operation Desert Storm.